1981

HELP YOUR CHILD
LEARN THE 3R'S
THROUGH ACTIVE PLAY

HELP YOUR CHILD
LEARN THE 3R'S
THROUGH ACTIVE PLAY

By

JAMES H. HUMPHREY

Professor of Physical Education
University of Maryland
College Park, Maryland

and

JOY N. HUMPHREY

Instructor
Prince George's County
Maryland Public Schools

CHARLES   C   THOMAS   •   PUBLISHER
Springfield   •   Illinois   •   U.S.A.

Published and Distributed Throughout the World by
CHARLES C THOMAS ● PUBLISHER
Bannerstone House
301-327 East Lawrence Avenue, Springfield, Illinois, U.S.A.

© *1980, by* CHARLES C THOMAS ● PUBLISHER
ISBN 0-398-04106-7
Library of Congress Catalog Card Number: 80-16979

With **THOMAS BOOKS** *careful attention is given to all details of*
manufacturing and design. It is the Publisher's desire to present books that
are satisfactory as to their physical qualities and artistic possibilities and
appropriate for their particular use. THOMAS BOOKS *will be true to those*
laws of quality that assure a good name and good will.

Printed in the United States of America
V-R-1

Library of Congress Cataloging in Publication Data
Humphrey, James Harry, 1911-
  Help your child learn the 3R's through active play.

  Includes index.
  1. Play. 2. Child development. 3. Language
arts (Primary) 4. Arithmetic--Study and teaching
(Primary) I. Humphrey, Joy N., joint author.
LB1137.H78   649'.68   80-16979
ISBN 0-398-04106-7

PREFACE

THE important role of active play in learning has been recognized for centuries. In fact, the idea of active play as a desirable learning medium has been traced to the ancient Egyptians. Through the ages some of the most profound thinkers in history have expounded positively in terms of the value of active play as a way of learning. This book provides a guide for parents on how to help their children learn through active play.

The book is concerned with the two very important current trends of *parenting* and the *back-to-basics* movement. Briefly, this means that through a very enjoyable parent-child relationship the child can learn about the basic 3R's. Over 175 active play experiences are provided with specific directions on how they can be used for this purpose. These activities have been thoroughly tested and have been found to be outstanding as learning experiences for children both at the preschool level as well as after they enter school.

A book is seldom the product of the authors alone. Admittedly, the authors do most of the things concerned with actually putting a book together, from the germ of the idea to eventually getting it published. However, it is almost always true that many individuals participate, at least indirectly, in some way before a book is finally "put to bed." This volume is no exception. To acknowledge everyone personally would be practically impossible. Therefore, we would like to acknowledge collectively the hundreds of parents, teachers, and children who participated so willingly in our experiments with the active play experiences, and thus made this final volume possible.

J.H.H.
J.N.H.

CONTENTS

HELP YOUR CHILD
LEARN THE 3R'S
THROUGH ACTIVE PLAY

Chapter One

A MESSAGE FOR PARENTS

THIS book is for parents. Its purpose is to help them help their children learn. The book is concerned mainly with the current trends that emphasize the importance of *parenting*, and the so-called *back-to-basics* movement.

Generally speaking, the book has two important functions. First, it can be used by parents to help their preschoolers get ready for school, and second, parents should find it valuable as a means of helping their children after they enter school.

School officials would like to get parents more involved in the education of their children. Moreover, most parents themselves want desperately to help their children cope with schoolwork. However, most are at a loss to know where to begin and how to proceed. The material presented in this book should go a long way in helping to meet this need because it provides information for parents on how they can assist their children in learning through the enjoyable process of active play.

LEARNING THROUGH ACTIVE PLAY

Although we will go into considerable detail in later chapters about child learning through active play, it seems appropriate to make some general comments about the approach at this point.

One of the most important characteristics of life is movement, and most of man's achievements are based upon his ability to move. Obviously, the very young child is not a highly intelligent being in the sense of abstract thinking, and he only gradually acquires the ability to deal with symbols and to intellectualize his experiences in the course of his development. Since the child is a creature of movement and feeling, any effort to educate him should take this dominance of movement into account.

Among the most important movement activities of children

are those which involve their active play experiences such as participation in active games, performing stunts, and other pleasurable physical activities. For centuries many of our best known thinkers have recognized that child learning takes well through active play. However, despite this knowledge, throughout the ages children have been expected to learn almost entirely under sedentary conditions, sitting still and listening. This is a most unfortunate situation, since it tends to violate much of what we know about child development. In fact, some scientists have recently reported that the traditional procedures for learning currently being imposed upon young children may possibly decrease their potential for learning at a later time.

Our own research over a period of several years has shown that by use of active play experiences, young children can learn to read, write, and develop understandings in mathematics. Compared with some of the traditional ways of teaching, this approach tends to enable them to learn better and retain what has been learned longer.

We are not suggesting that this be the only procedure used, but that greater consideration be given to the natural urge for active play as a way of learning because it is so consistent with the developmental needs of children. This approach is particularly appropriate for parents, because it provides them with a way to help their children learn under the enjoyable conditions of active play.

PARENTS AS TEACHERS

For many years schools have tended to assume more and more responsibility not only for the education of children but also for their social development. While it could be argued that there is merit in this approach, at the same time there appears to be a welcome trend to get parents more involved as far as child learning is concerned. The reason for this is obvious: parents should be considered helpers rather than as unconcerned onlookers in the educational development of their children.

Evidence for this trend is shown in the growing effort in

many parts of the country to try to increase academic achievement of children by teaching parents to teach their children at home. Increasing numbers of seminars and workshops are being held for this purpose. The effectiveness of such programs is shown in national surveys that indicate that children whose parents used home-learning activities made greater progress in school than those children who did not benefit from such help.

Education is as much the business of the home as of the school, because it is obvious that the school alone does not educate the child. Yet, many parents believe that a child begins to learn only when he enters school. They do not seem to realize that they are not only the child's first teacher but probably the most important one the child will ever have.

Parents can and should help prepare their children before they enter school and also assist their children with schoolwork after they are in school. An abundance of evidence is being accumulated to support this idea. For example, one national survey has shown that preschool children receiving help from their parents perform better than those who do not receive such attention.

There are many valid reasons why this is true. Research in child development indicates that the direction of a child's mental development is likely to be determined between ten months and one and one-half years of age. In addition, the human learning patterns can become well established by age three. Consequently, the action that parents take in helping their children is extremely important. Moreover, most authorities in the area of child development tend to feel that the first five years are the most important formative ones in the child's life. The child's ability to learn various skills in these formative years before he enters school may depend a good bit on the extent to which his parents provide him with desirable and worthwhile learning experiences.

It has been estimated that of the approximately three and one-half million children entering first grade, more than 400,000 of them will be asked to repeat that grade. It has been further estimated that if present trends continue, one-fourth of current first grade children, by the time they reach the age of eleven, will be reading two or more years below grade level. In fact, school officials of one large city system recently reported that about 50 percent of its students were dropping out of school at the ninth grade level because inability to read would prevent them from graduating from high school.

It is easy to blame the schools for this sad state of affairs. However, before doing so we might well take another look at the responsibility of parents as important helpers in the education of their children. (We reiterate the important function of this book in helping to improve upon some of the conditions mentioned above.)

SOME COMMENTS ABOUT THE BASICS

We have already mentioned that this book is concerned with the *back-to-basics* movement. Certainly, this is indicated in the title of the book. The subjects of reading, writing, and mathematics (reading, 'riting, and 'rithmetic), familiarly known as the "3R's," are *basic* to the education of everyone. The authors tend to think of these as the subjects of *communication and computation.* In reading, others communicate their thoughts and feelings to us through the printed or written page. Writing is one means we use (the other is speaking) to communicate our thoughts and feelings to others. Certain aspects of mathematics are needed to determine such things as amounts and reckoning (computation).

In recent years parents have tended to feel that there has been a serious neglect of the 3R's. On the other hand, many school officials contend that this criticism is not justified. They base this on the notion that schools have not necessarily neglected the basics but that they may be approaching the study of them in a different manner.

In any event, the hard fact is that averages in national test scores, such as the Scholastic Aptitude Test (SAT), have been declining over a period of years. Some of the reasons given for this are (1) these tests contain cultural biases that put minority students at a disadvantage; (2) there is less emphasis on reading and mathematics skills in elementary and secondary schools; and (3) the influence of television tends to draw students away from the more traditional activities of reading and studying.

The extent to which these reasons are true is accepted by some and rejected by others. It is interesting to note that more than four-fifths of the nation's school board members believe that the public schools should put greater emphasis on reading and writing and mathematics skills, according to a recent National School Boards Association survey. Of the 600 school board members responding to this survey, only one in ten felt that there is adequate stress put on the 3R's now, while only 1 percent thought that basic skills are being given too much emphasis.

One of the interesting things about the approach recommended in this book is that it not only gives parents an opportunity to help their children with the *basics* but at the same time it makes use of a *basic* need of children — *active play!* Through this approach children can learn and improve upon the basic skills in a manner that is enjoyable to both the parent and the child.

AN OVERVIEW OF THE CONTENT OF THE BOOK

It seems appropriate at this point to give the reader a general idea of the content of the book. There are two major reasons for this. First, the reader can get a quick idea of the information contained in the book, and second, it should make for greater ease in reading the individual chapters.

Throughout the book we have used educational terms. In practically all instances an effort has been made to give a clear and relatively simple meaning of these terms. A good feature about this is that a parent who has some idea of the meaning of terms used in educational circles should feel more comfortable in dealing with teachers when conferring with them about a child's schoolwork.

Having read this far, you should be aware that the function of this introductory chapter is to acquaint the parent in a general way with what the book is all about. The following discussion is intended to give a more detailed account of the content of each chapter.

Chapter Two is intended to familiarize the reader with the

various aspects of development of young children. Although it is granted that most parents should understand their own children better than anyone else, many parents are not necessarily aware of the many factors concerned with child development. For this reason we feel that some general information along these lines can be of value. Therefore, consideration is given to the identification of certain developmental traits and characteristics of children of immediate preschool ages as well as children in the early school years. In addition, attention is given to sex differences with reference to success of boys and girls in school. Also taken into account in this chapter is a discussion of child learning, along with application of this to active play.

In Chapter Three attention is directed to the subject of *why* children can learn through active play. Many people associate learning only with work and can hardly conceive of how learning can take place through play. It is mainly for this reason that we provide a discussion of the basic theory underlying the active play way of learning. Included is an account of why the active play learning medium is closely related to how children develop, along with a discussion of such factors as motivation, fun and emotional release, and the muscle sense aspect of the active play learning medium.

Chapter Four is concerned with ways to improve upon ability to learn through active play. A number of factors that can interfere with a child's ability to learn are identified and discussed, along with how a deficiency in any of these can detract from learning. There is also an account of how the parent can tell if there is such a deficiency, and active play experiences are recommended to help improve upon it.

In the fifth chapter detailed information is provided to show how the parent can help the child learn to read through active play. Also discussed are ways to help children to improve their reading ability once they have started to read. This discussion includes how to determine a child's readiness to read, how to improve upon reading skills, and how to improve upon comprehension through this medium. Another interesting feature presented in this chapter is the APAV technique to help children learn to read. This procedure should be a welcome one for those parents who like to spend time reading to their children.

Chapter Six interprets the meaning of the "old and new math" with emphasis upon modern attempts to provide for the best of both. Consideration is given to how parents can help the child through active play with such concepts as numbers and numeration systems, operations of arithmetic (addition-subtraction-multiplication-division), geometric figures, linear and liquid measurements, telling time, and coin recognition. Also presented is a technique for integrating listening and reading experiences and mathematics for the purpose of developing mathematics concepts.

The final chapter is concerned with writing readiness and writing problems. The meaning of manuscript and cursive writing is explained along with how the parent can help the child with these. There is a discussion of how active play experiences can be put into writing along with an explanation of how children can learn to write through active play.

HOW TO USE THE BOOK

Since this is essentially a "How to" book it seems appropriate to make some recommendations for its use. The following list of recommendations is suggestive only, because each indivdiual reader will eventually make his or her own decision as to how best use of the book can be obtained. The guidelines submitted here should be viewed with this idea in mind.

1. Read the entire book before attempting to make application of the material that it contains. This should be helpful in providing the reader with an overall understanding of learning through active play.

2. There are numerous ways to use the many play activities contained in the book. In many instances the parent can use a one-to-one relationship with the child. In situations where more than two participants are involved, other family members can engage in the activities. The child can be the *principal* player under these conditions. Also, groups of parents may wish to cooperate in a kind of active play learning neighborhood undertaking.

3. Be sure that you know the activity thoroughly before you attempt to teach it to the child. If any material or equipment is necessary it should be readily available.
4. Make sure the child is having fun in the performance of the activity. If you recognize that it is ceasing to be fun, you can stop and perhaps change to another activity.
5. Be alert to recognize fatigue symptoms in the child. Regardless of how exciting a learning activity may be, little or no learning is likely to take place when a child has become fatigued.
6. The time of day to conduct the activities is very important. For preschool children, about midmorning is a good time. Parents may wish to set aside a certain time each day for these activities. On the other hand, it can be very effective when an experience develops in a more or less spontaneous manner. With school age children each individual parent will no doubt find the most suitable time for the activities. Ordinarily, it is not considered a good practice to engage the child in anything related to school immediately when he returns home from school.
7. Give the child praise for performance. Such positive reinforcement is likely to inspire him to want to continue with the experience.
8. Try to structure the active play learning experience in such a way as to allow the child to succeed. Too many children have too many failures early in life. Thus, it is most important that children have a feeling of success so as to build confidence in themselves.

The suggestions set forth consist of only a few of the possibilities for use of the book. Each individual reader will find numerous other ways to apply the material.

Over 2,300 years ago the Greek philosopher Plato suggested that all early education should be a sort of play and should develop around play situations. We are confident that you will find this to be true in modern times as you experiment with active play as a way to help your child learn.

CHILD DEVELOPMENT AND LEARNING

IT was mentioned previously that most parents should understand their own children better than anyone else. However, simply recognizing a child's mannerisms and his likes and dislikes does not necessarily mean that a parent has a full understanding of child development and learning. In fact, even those professional workers who spend their time studying about children are not always in complete agreement with regard to the complex nature of child development. The major purpose of this chapter is to present general information on this subject. This means that the discussion will be concerned with the so-called "average" child. It should be remembered that averages tend to be arrived at mathematically and that a child develops at his own individual rate. It is quite likely that a child may be above average in some characteristics and below average in others. It is important that parents realize this; thus, the material in this chapter should be considered with this idea in mind.

MEANING OF TERMS

To avoid confusion, it seems appropriate for us to convey to the reader the meaning of certain terms used in this chapter. The two major terms that we are concerned with are *development* and *learning*.

Development is concerned with changes in the child's ability to function at an increasingly higher level. For example, a stage in development in the infant is from creeping to crawling. This is later followed by the developmental stage of walking when the child moves to an upright position and begins to propel himself over the surface area by putting one foot in front of the other.

Most definitions of *learning* are characterized by the idea that it involves some sort of change in the individual. This means

11

that when an individual has learned, his behavior is modified in one or more ways. Thus, a good standard for learning would be that after having an experience a person could behave in a way in which he could not have behaved before having had the experience. In this general connection, many learning theorists suggest that it is not possible to *see* learning. However, behavior can be seen, and when a change in behavior has occurred, then it is possible to infer that change and learning have occurred. This concept is depicted in the following diagram.

Learning Can be Inferred by a Change in Behavior

CHILD BEHAVES IN A GIVEN WAY	→	CHILD IS IN A LEARNING SITUATION	→	CHILD BEHAVES IN A WAY THAT IS DIFFERENT FROM BEFORE HE WAS IN THE LEARNING SITUATION

The essential difference *between* development and learning is that development deals with general abilities while learning is concerned with specific behaviors.

When it is considered that development of children brings about needs, and that these needs must be met satisfactorily, the importance of an understanding of development is readily seen. When an understanding of the various aspects of development is accomplished, parents are then in a better position to provide improved procedures for meeting the needs of their children. This implies that parents might well be guided by what could be called a developmental philosophy if they are to meet with any degree of success in their dealings with their children.

TOTAL PERSONALITY DEVELOPMENT

Total development is the fundamental purpose of the education of children. All attempts at such education should take into account a combination of *physical, social, emotional,* and *intellectual* aspects of human behavior. Thus, these are the forms of development that we will consider in our discussion here. Of course, there are other forms of development, but they can be subclassified under one of these areas. For example, *motor development*, which has been described as progressive change in motor performance, is considered as a part of the broader aspect of *physical development*. In addition, *moral development*, which is concerned with the capacity of the individual to distinguish between standards of right and wrong, could be considered a dimension of the broad aspect of *social development*. This is to say that moral development involving achievement in ability to determine right from wrong is influential in the individual's social behavior.

A great deal of clinical and experimental evidence indicates that a human being must be considered as a *whole* and not a collection of parts. For purposes here we would prefer to use the term *total personality* in referring to the child as a unified individual or total being. Perhaps a more common term is *whole child*. However, the term *total personality* is commonly used in the field of psychology, and it has recently been gaining more use in the field of education. Moreover, when we consider it from a point of view of man existing as a person, it is interesting to note that "existence as a person" is one rather common definition of personality.

The total personality consists of the sum of all the physical, social, emotional, and intellectual aspects of any individual, i.e. the major forms of development previously identified. The total personality is *one thing* comprising these various major aspects. All of these components are highly interrelated and interdependent. All are of importance to the balance and health of the personality because only in terms of the health of each can the personality as a whole maintain a completely healthful state. The condition of any one aspect affects each other aspect to a degree and thus the personality as a whole.

When a nervous child stutters or becomes nauseated, a mental state is *not* necessarily causing a physical symptom. On the contrary, a pressure imposed upon the organism causes a series of reactions that include thought, verbalization, digestive processes, and muscular function. It is not that the mind causes the body to become upset; the total organism is upset by a situation and reflects its upset in several ways, including disturbance in thought, feeling, and bodily processes. The whole individual responds in interaction with the social and physical environment, and as the individual is affected by the environment, he or she, in turn, has an effect upon it.

However, because of long tradition during which physical development *or* intellectual development, rather than physical *and* intellectual development, has been glorified, we are often still accustomed to dividing the two in our thinking. The result may be that we sometimes pull human beings apart with this kind of thinking.

Traditional attitudes that separate the mind and body tend to lead to unbalanced development of the child with respect to mind and body and/or social adjustment. What is more important is that we fail to use the strengths of one to serve the needs of the other.

The foregoing statements have attempted to point out rather forcefully the idea that the identified components of the total personality comprise the unified individual. That each of these aspects might well be considered separately should also be taken into account. As such, each aspect should warrant a separate discussion. This appears extremely important if one is to understand fully the place of each aspect as an integral part of the total personality. The following discussions of the physical, social, emotional, and intellectual aspects of personality should be viewed in this general frame of reference.

THE PHYSICAL ASPECT OF PERSONALITY

One point of departure in discussing the physical aspect of personality could be to state that "everybody has a body." Some are short, some are tall, some are lean, and some are fat. Children come in different sizes, but all of them have a certain innate capacity that is influenced by the environment.

It might be said of the child that he *is* his body. It is something he can see. It is his base of operation — or what might be termed the *physical base*. The other components of the total personality — social, emotional, and intellectual — are somewhat vague as far as the child is concerned. Although these are manifested in various ways, children do not always see them as they do the physical aspect. Consequently, it becomes all important that a child be helped early in life to gain control over the physical aspect, or what is known as basic body control. The ability to do this, of course, will vary from one child to another. It will likely depend upon the status of *physical fitness* of the child. The broad area of physical fitness can be broken down into certain components, and it is important that individuals achieve to the best of their natural ability as far as these components are concerned. There is not complete agreement as far as identification of the components of physical fitness are concerned. However, the President's Council on Physical Fitness and Sports considers these components to consist of the following:

1. Muscular strength (the contraction power of the muscles).
2. Muscular endurance (ability of the muscles to perform work).
3. Circulatory-respiratory endurance (moderate contractions of large muscle groups for relatively long periods of time).
4. Muscular power (ability to release maximum muscular force in the shortest time).
5. Agility (speed in changing direction, or body position).
6. Speed (rapidity with which successive movements of the same kind can be performed).
7. Flexibility (range of movement in a joint or a sequence of joints).
8. Balance (ability to maintain position and equilibrium).
9. Coordination (working together of the muscles in the performance of a specific task).

The components of physical fitness and, thus, the physical aspect of personality can be measured by precise instruments, such as measurements of muscular strength. Moreover, we can tell how tall a child is or how heavy he or she is at any stage of his or her development. In addition, medically trained personnel can derive other accurate information with assessments of blood pressure, blood counts, and urinalysis.

THE SOCIAL ASPECT OF PERSONALITY

Human beings are social beings. They work together for the benefit of society. They have fought together in time of national emergencies to preserve the kind of society they believe in, and they play together. While all this may be true, the social aspect of personality still is quite vague and confusing particularly as far as children are concerned.

It was a relatively easy matter to identify certain components of physical fitness such as strength and endurance. However, this does not necessarily hold true for components of social fitness. The components of physical fitness are the same for children as for adults. On the other hand, the components of social fitness for children may be different from the components of social fitness for adults. By some adult standards children might be considered as social misfits because certain behavior of children might not be socially acceptable to some adults.

To the dismay of some parents, young children are uninhibited as far as the social aspect of personality is concerned. In this regard we need to be concerned with social maturity as it pertains to the growing and ever-changing child. We need to give consideration to certain characteristics of social maturity and how well they are dealt with at the different stages of child development.

Perhaps parents need to ask themselves such questions as: Am I helping my child to become self-reliant by giving him or her independence at the proper time? Am I helping him or her to be outgoing and interested in others as well as in himself or herself? Am I helping my child to know how to satisfy his or her own needs in a socially desirable way?

THE EMOTIONAL ASPECT OF PERSONALITY

For many years, emotion has been a difficult concept to define; in addition, there have been many changing ideas and theories as far as the study of emotion is concerned.

Obviously, it is not the purpose of a book of this nature to attempt to go into any great depth on a subject that has been one of the most intricate undertakings of psychology for many years. A few general statements relative to the nature of emotion do appear to be in order, however, if we are to understand more clearly this aspect of personality.

Emotion may be described as a response a person makes to a stimulus for which he is not prepared, or which suggests a possible source of gain or loss for him. For example, if a child is confronted with a situation and does not have a satisfactory response, the emotional pattern of fear may result. If one finds himself or herself in a position where desires are frustrated, the emotional pattern of anger may occur.

This line of thought suggests that emotions might be classified in two different ways — those which are *pleasant* and those which are *unpleasant*. For example, *joy* could be considered a pleasant emotional experience while *fear* would be an unpleasant one. It is interesting to note that a good proportion of the literature is devoted to emotions that are unpleasant. It has been found that in psychology books much more space is given to such emotional patterns as fear and anger than to such pleasant emotions as joy and contentment.

Generally speaking, the pleasantness or unpleasantness of an emotion seems to be determined by its strength or intensity, by the nature of the situation arousing it, and by the way an individual perceives or interprets the situation. As far as young children are concerned, their emotions tend to be more intense than those of adults. If a parent is not aware of this aspect of child behavior, he or she will not likely understand why a child may react rather violently to a situation that to the parent seems somewhat insignificant. It should also be taken into account that different children will react differently to the same type of situation. For example, something that might anger one person might have a rather passive influence on another individual. In this regard, it is interesting to observe the effect that winning or losing has on certain children.

THE INTELLECTUAL ASPECT OF PERSONALITY

The word *intelligence* is derived from the Latin word *intellectus*, which literally means the "power of knowing." Intelligence has been described in many ways. One general description of it is the "capacity to learn or understand."

Individuals possess varying degrees of intelligence, and most people fall within a range of what is called "normal" intelligence. In dealing with this aspect of personality we should perhaps give attention to what might be considered some components of intellectual fitness. However, this is a difficult thing to do. Because of the somewhat vague nature of intelligence, it is practically impossible to identify specific components of it. Thus, we need to view intellectual fitness in a somewhat different manner.

For purposes of this discussion we would like to consider intellectual fitness from two different, but closely related, points of view: first, from a standpoint of intellectual *needs* and second, from a standpoint of how certain things *influence* intelligence. It might be said that if a child's intellectual needs are being met then perhaps we could also say that he or she is intellectually fit. From the second point of view, if we know how certain things influence intelligence then we might understand better how to contribute to intellectual fitness by improving upon these factors.

There appears to be some rather general agreement with regard to the intellectual needs of children. Among others, these needs include (1) a need for challenging experiences at the child's level of ability, (2) a need for intellectually successful and satisfying experiences, (3) a need for the opportunity to solve problems, and (4) a need for the opportunity to participate in creative experiences instead of always having to conform.

Some of the factors that tend to influence intelligence are (1) health and physical condition, (2) emotional disturbance, and (3) certain social and economic factors.

When parents have a realization of intellectual needs and factors influencing intelligence, perhaps then, and only then, can they deal satisfactorily with their children in helping them in their intellectual pursuits.

It was mentioned that an important intellectual need for children is the opportunity to participate in creative experiences. This need is singled out for special mention because the opportunities for creative experiences are perhaps more evident in active play situations than in almost any other single aspect of the child's life.

DEVELOPMENTAL CHARACTERISTICS OF CHILDREN

It is important that parents have a general overview of the behavior of children as they progress in their development. This is the intent of the following discussion.

The range of age levels from six through eight usually includes children from grades one through three. A child is considered a preschooler if he or she is below age six unless the school system supports a kindergarten. In this case the child would enter school at approximately age five.

In our culture when the child begins his formal education he leaves home and family for a part of the day to take his place with a group of children of approximately the same age. Not only is he taking an important step in becoming increasingly more independent and self-reliant, but as he learns he moves from being a highly self-centered individual to becoming a more socialized group member.

This stage is characterized by a certain lack of motor coordination, because the small muscles of the hands and fingers are not as well developed as the large muscles of the arms and legs. Thus, as he starts his formal education, the child uses large crayons or pencils as a means of expressing himself. His urge to action is expressed through movement and noise. Children at these age levels thrive on vigorous activity. They develop as they climb, run, jump, or keep time to music. An important physical aspect at this level is that the eyeball is increasing in size and the eye muscles are developing. This is an important factor in the child's readiness to see and read small print.

Even though he has a relatively short attention span, he is extremely curious about his environment. At this stage the parent can capitalize upon the child's urge to learn by providing opportunities for him to gain firsthand experiences through the use of the senses. He sees, hears, smells, feels, tastes, and of course plays in order to learn.

As the child progresses through various stages in his or her development, certain distinguishing characteristics can be identified, which provide implications for parental guidance.

The detailed description of the characteristics given here includes the age levels five through eight. It should be understood that these characteristics are suggestive of the behavior patterns of the so-called "normal" child. This implies that if a child does not conform to these characteristics, it should not be interpreted to mean that he or she is seriously deviating from the normal. In other words, it should be recognized by the parent that each child progresses at his or her own rate and that there can be much overlapping of the characteristics listed for each age level. A case in point is the range of heights and weights given in the following detailed lists of characteristics. These heights and weights are what might be called "a range within a range" and are computed averages within larger ranges. In other words, children at a given age level could possibly weigh much more or less and be much taller or shorter than the ranges indicate.

Characteristics of Five-Year-Old Children

Physical Characteristics

1. Boys' height, 42 to 46 inches; weight, 38 to 49 pounds; girls' height, 42 to 46 inches; weight 36 to 48 pounds.
2. May grow 2 or 3 inches and gain from 3 to 6 pounds during the year.
3. Girls may be about a year ahead of boys in physiological development.
4. Beginning to have better control of body.
5. The large muscles are better developed than the small muscles that control the fingers and hands.
6. Usually determined whether he will be right or left-handed.
7. Eye-hand coordination is not complete.
8. May have farsighted vision.
9. Vigorous and noisy, but activity appears to have definite direction.
10. Tires easily and needs plenty of rest.

Social Characteristics

1. Interest in neighborhood games that involve any number of children.

2. Plays various games to test his skills.
3. Enjoys other children and likes to be with them.
4. Interests are largely self-centered.
5. Seems to get along best in small groups.
6. Shows an interest in home activities.
7. Imitates when he plays.
8. Gets along well in taking turns.
9. Respects the belongings of other people.

Emotional Characteristics

1. Seldom shows jealousy toward younger siblings.
2. Usually sees only one way to do a thing.
3. Usually sees only one answer to a question.
4. Inclined not to change plans in the middle of an activity, but would rather begin over.
5. May fear being deprived of mother.
6. Some definite personality traits evidenced.
7. Is learning to get along better, but still may resort to quarreling and fighting.
8. Likes to be trusted with errands.
9. Enjoys performing simple tasks.
10. Wants to please and do what is expected of him.
11. Is beginning to sense right and wrong in terms of specific situations.

Intellectual Characteristics

1. Enjoys copying designs, letters, and numbers.
2. Interested in completing tasks.
3. May tend to monopolize table conversation.
4. Memory for past events good.
5. Looks at books and pretends to read.
6. Likes recordings, words, and music that tell a story.
7. Enjoys counting objects.
8. Over 2,000 words in speaking vocabulary.
9. Can speak in complete sentences.
10. Can sing simple melodies, beat good rhythms, and recognize simple tunes.

11. Daydreams seem to center around make-believe play.
12. Attention span increasing up to twenty minutes in some cases.
13. Is able to plan activities.
14. Enjoys stories, dramatic play, and games.
15. Enjoys making up dances to music.
16. Pronunciation is usually clear.
17. Can express his needs well in words.

Characteristics of Six-Year-Old Children

Physical Characteristics

1. Boys' height, 44 to 48 inches; weight, 41 to 54 pounds; girls' height, 43 to 48 inches; weight, 40 to 53 pounds.
2. Growth is gradual in weight and height.
3. Good supply of energy.
4. Marked activity urge absorbs him in running, jumping, chasing, and dodging games.
5. Muscular control becoming more effective with large objects.
6. There is a noticeable change in the eye-hand behavior.
7. Legs lengthening rapidly.
8. Big muscles crave activity.

Social Characteristics

1. Self-centered and has need for praise.
2. Likes to be first.
3. Indifferent to sex distinction.
4. Enjoys group play when groups tend to be small.
5. Likes parties but behavior may not always be acceptable to adults.
6. The majority enjoy school association and have a desire to learn.
7. Interested in conduct of his friends.
8. Boys like to fight and wrestle with peers to prove masculinity.
9. Shows an interest in group approval.

Emotional Characteristics

1. Restless and may have difficulty in making decisions.
2. Emotional pattern of anger may be difficult to control at times.
3. Behavior patterns may often be explosive and unpredictable.
4. Jealousy toward siblings at times; at other times takes pride in siblings.
5. Greatly excited by anything new.
6. Behavior becomes susceptible to shifts in direction, inwardly motivated and outwardly stimulated.
7. May be self-assertive and dramatic.

Intellectual Characteristics

1. Speaking vocabulary of over 2,500 words.
2. Interest span inclined to be short.
3. Can learn number combinations making up to ten.
4. Can learn comparative values of the common coins.
5. Can define simple objects in terms of what they are used for.
6. Can learn difference between right and left side of body.
7. Has an association with creative activity and motorized life experiences.
8. Drawings are crude but realistic and suggestive of early man.
9. Will contribute to guided group planning.
10. Conversation usually concerns his own experiences and interests.
11. Curiosity is active and memory is strong.
12. Identifies himself with imaginary characters.

Characteristics of Seven-Year-Old Children

Physical Characteristics

1. Boys' height, 46 to 51 inches; weight, 45 to 60 pounds; girls' height, 46 to 50 inches; weight, 44 to 59 pounds.

2. Big muscle activity predominates in interest and value.
3. More improvement in eye-hand coordination.
4. May grow 2 or 3 inches and gain 3 to 5 pounds in weight during the year.
5. Tires easily and shows fatigue in the afternoon.
6. Has slow reaction time.
7. Heart and lungs are smallest in proportion to body size.
8. General health may be precarious, with susceptibility to disease high and resistance low.
9. Endurance is relatively low.
10. Coordination is improving with throwing and catching becoming more accurate.
11. Whole-body movements are under better control.
12. Small accessory muscles developing.
13. Displays amazing amounts of vitality.

Social Characteristics

1. Wants recognition for his individual achievements.
2. Sex differences are not of very great importance.
3. Not always a good loser.
4. Conversation often centers around family.
5. Learning to stand up for his own rights.
6. Interested in friends and is not influenced by their social or economic status.
7. May have nervous habits such as nail biting, tongue sucking, scratching, or pulling at ear.
8. Attaining orientation in time.
9. Gets greater enjoyment from group play.
10. Shows greater signs of cooperative efforts.

Emotional Characteristics

1. Curiosity and creative desires may condition responses.
2. May be difficult to take criticism from adults.
3. Wants to be more independent.
4. Reaching for new experiences and trying to relate himself to enlarged world.
5. Overanxious to reach goals set by parents and teachers.

6. Critical of himself and sensitive to failure.
7. Emotional pattern of anger is more controlled.
8. Becoming less impulsive and boisterous in actions than at six.

Intellectual Characteristics

1. Abstract thinking is barely beginning.
2. Is able to listen longer.
3. Reads some books by himself.
4. Is able to reason, but has little experience upon which to base judgments.
5. The attention span is still short and retention poor, but does not object to repetition.
6. Reaction time is still slow.
7. Learning to evaluate the achievements of self and others.
8. Concerned with own lack of skill and achievement.
9. Becoming more realistic and less imaginative.

Characteristics of Eight-Year-Old Children

Physical Characteristics

1. Boys' height, 48 to 53 inches; weight, 49 to 70 pounds; girls' height, 48 to 52 inches; weight, 47 to 66 pounds.
2. Interested in games requiring coordination of small muscles.
3. Arms are lengthening and hands are growing larger.
4. Eyes can accommodate more easily.
5. Some develop poor posture.
6. Accidents appear to occur more frequently at this age.
7. Appreciates correct skill performance.

Social Characteristics

1. Girls may be more careful of their clothes than boys.
2. Leaves many things uncompleted.
3. Has special friends.
4. Has longer periods of peaceful play.

5. Does not like playing alone.
6. Enjoys dramatizing.
7. Starts collections.
8. Enjoys school and dislikes staying home.
9. Likes variety.
10. Recognition of property rights is well established.
11. Responds well to group activity.
12. Interest will focus on friends of own sex.
13. Beginning of the desire to become a member of the club.

Emotional Characteristics

1. Dislikes taking much criticism from adults.
2. Can give and take criticism in his own group.
3. May develop enemies.
4. Does not like to be treated as a child.
5. Has a marked sense of humor.
6. First impulse is to blame others.
7. Becoming more realistic and wants to find out for himself.

Intellectual Characteristics

1. Can tell day of month and year.
2. Voluntary attention span is increasing.
3. Interested in far-off places, and ways of communication now have real meaning.
4. Becoming more aware of adult world and his place in it.
5. Ready to tackle almost anything.
6. Shows a capacity for self-evaluation.
7. Likes to memorize.
8. Not always too good at telling time, but very much aware of it.

Perhaps the best source of *needs* and *interests* of children is their physical, social, emotional, and intellectual characteristics. Thus, the preceding information could serve as a general guide for parents in their attempts to deal with their children's needs and interests.

SEX DIFFERENCES IN EARLY SCHOOL SUCCESS

After a critical examination of the preceding developmental characteristics of children, it can be seen that there are few appreciable differences between boys and girls in the five to eight year age range. Granted, there are certain differences, but they are not as nearly pronounced as in the later years. It is interesting to note, however, that many people have been critical of the early school learning environment, particularly as far as boys are concerned. Some of these critics have gone so far as to say that young boys are being discriminated against in their early school years. Let us examine the premise.

We have already stated that a generally accepted description of the term *learning* is that it involves some sort of change in *behavior*. Many learning theorists maintain that behavior is a product of heredity and environment. Unquestionably, it is very apparent that environment plays a major role in determining one's behavior. B. F. Skinner, the renowned Harvard University learning theorist, has said that man is indeed controlled by his environment. Nevertheless, we must remember that it is an environment largely of his own making. The issue here is whether or not an environment is provided that is best suited for learning for boys at the early school grade levels.

While the school has no control over ancestry, it can, within certain limitations, exercise some degree of control over the kind of environment in which the learner must function. Generally speaking, it is doubtful that all schools have provided an environment that is most conducive to learning as far as young boys are concerned. In fact, many child development specialists have characterized the environment at the primary level of education as *feminized*.

The biological differences between boys and girls in this particular age range should be considered, and it is questionable whether educational planning has always taken these important differences into account. Over the years there has been an accumulation of evidence on this general subject appearing in the literature on child development, some of which will be summarized here.

Due to certain male hormonal conditions, boys tend to be more aggressive, restless, and impatient. In addition, the male has more rugged bone and muscular structure and, as a consequence, greater strength than the female at all ages. Because of this, males tend to display greater muscular reactivity, which in turn expresses itself in a stronger tendency toward restlessness and vigorous overt activity. This condition is concerned with the greater oxygen consumption required to fulfill the male's need for increased energy production. The male organism might be compared to an engine that operates at higher levels of speed and intensity than the less energetic female organism. Several years ago Dr. Franklin Henry of the University of California at Berkeley found in his research that, on average, males have what might be called an "active response set," whereas females might have a "reactive response set." This could be interpreted to mean that males confront the environment with an activity orientation, while females have a response orientation.

Another factor to take into account is the difference in Basal Metabolic Rate (BMR) in young boys and girls. The BMR is indicative of the speed at which body fuel is changed to energy, as well as how fast this energy is used. The BMR can be measured in terms of calories per meter of body surface with a calorie representing a unit measure of heat energy in food. It has been found that, on average, BMR rises from birth to about three years of age and then starts to decline until the ages of approximately twenty to twenty-four. The BMR is higher for boys than for girls, particularly at the early age levels. Because of the higher BMR, boys will in turn have a higher amount of energy to expend. Because of differences in sex hormone conditions and Basal Metabolic Rate, it appears logical to assume that these factors will influence the male in his behavior patterns.

From a growth and development point of view, while at birth the female is from 1/2 to 1 centimeter less in length than the male and around 300 grams less in weight, she is actually a much better developed organism. It is estimated on the average that at the time of entrance into school, the female is usually six to twelve months more physically mature than the male. As a result, girls may be likely to learn earlier how to perform such tasks of manual dexterity as buttoning their clothing. In one of our own observational studies of preschool children it was found that little girls were able to perform the task of tying their shoestrings at a rate of almost four times that of little boys.

Although all schools should not be categorized in the same manner, many of them have been captured by the dead hand of tradition and ordinarily provide an environment that places emphasis upon such factors as neatness, orderliness, and passiveness, all of which are easier for girls to conform to than boys. Of course, this may be partly because our culture has forced females to be identified with many of these characteristics.

The authoritarian and sedentary classroom atmosphere that prevails in some schools and that involves the "sit still and listen" syndrome fails to take into account the greater activity drive and physical aggressiveness of boys. What have been characterized as feminization traits prevailing in many elementary schools tend to have an adverse influence on the young male child as far as learning is concerned.

Some studies have shown that as far as hyperactivity (overactive) is concerned, boys may outnumber girls by a ratio of as much as nine to one. This may be one of the reasons why teachers generally tend to rate young males as being so much more aggressive than females with the result that young boys are considered to be more negative and extraverted. Because of these characteristics, boys generally have poorer relationships with their teachers than do girls, and in the area of behavior problems and discipline in the age range from five to eight, boys account for twice as many disturbances as girls. The importance of this factor is borne out when it is considered that good teacher-pupil relationships tend to raise the achievement level of both sexes.

Various studies have shown that girls generally receive higher grades than boys even though boys may achieve as well as and, in some instances, better than girls. It is also clearly evident that boys in the early years fail twice as often as girls even when there is no significant difference between intelligence and achievement test scores of both sexes. This suggests that even though both sexes have the same intellectual tools, there are other factors that are against learning as far as boys are concerned.

If one is willing to accept the research findings and observational evidence appearing in the child development literature regarding the premise outlined here, then the question is: "What attempts, if any, are being made to improve the condition?" At one time it was thought that the solution might lie in defeminization of the schools at the early age levels by putting more men into classrooms. This apparently has met with little success because the learning environment remains essentially the same regardless of the sex of the teacher. Some educators have suggested that little boys start to school later or that little girls start earlier. The problem with this, of course, is that state laws concerned with school entrance are likely to distinguish only in terms of age and not sex. In a few remote instances some schools have experimented with separating boys and girls at the early grade levels. In some cases this form of grouping has resulted in both groups achieving at a higher level than when the sexes were in classes together.

The major question that must be posed is: "What can be done to at least partially restructure an environment that will be more favorable to the learning of young boys?" One step in this direction recommended by various child development specialists is to develop curriculum content that is more *action* oriented, thus taking into account the basic need for motor activity involved in human movement. Deep consideration might well be given to learning activities through which excess energy, especially of boys, can be used. One step in the implimentation of this recommendation could be to give more consideration to the active play learning medium.

Lest the reader be concerned that we are recommending that children go to school to play all the time, we are not suggesting that the environment be restructured to include *only* this kind of procedure. However, it might well be considered, particularly at those times when young children become exceedingly restless in a sedentary learning situation. Thus, we are not suggesting that this be the only procedure used but that some consideration be given to the natural urge for body movement as a way of learning, because it is so consistent with the developmental needs of children. While it is not likely that this approach will be used to a great extent in the schools, it can be very effective when applied in the home situation.

The above discussion is not intended to imply that the active play learning approach should be used only for young boys. Although our research shows that it may be more favorable for boys, at the same time it provides a very desirable medium of learning for both preschool girls and those in their early school years. The reader should also remember — and we want to point this out very forcefully — that the preceding discussion is based on the so-called average boy or girl. Obviously, because of individual differences in children, both boys and girls will possibly deviate from the standards reported here.

THE NATURE OF LEARNING

The learning process is complicated and complex, and the task of explaining it has occupied the attention of psychologists for many years. In recent years this effort has been intensified, and more about learning is being discovered almost daily. It is not our intent to try to go into depth on anything as complicated as the learning process. On the other hand, it will be our purpose to make some generalized statements about it as well as to consider certain conditions under which learning is best likely to take place. The reason for this is that, although it is not definitely known what happens when learning takes place, a great deal is known about conditions under which it can take place most effectively.

The word *learning* is used in many connections. For example, we speak of learning how to walk, how to speak, how to make a living, and how to feel about various things such as failing, aggressiveness, going to school, and so forth. As has been mentioned previously, whatever kind of learning one is concerned with, specialists seem to agree that it involves some kind of change in behavior. Obviously, our concern here is with changes in behavior that are brought about by child-parent relationships with particular reference to active play.

Just what does change in behavior mean? This is an extremely important question because it suggests that the child
proceeds promptly to behave in a certain way as a result of a
child-parent interaction in an active play situation. The word
behavior can refer to improved understandings as reflected ver-
bally and/or in writing. Thus, even though a child cannot
always change his or her behavior in terms of practical performance and actually *do* what he or she has learned, the child can
reflect greater understanding in written or spoken verbal behavior. Moreover, he or she can reflect it in contrived classroom
situations where he or she is able to act as though the improved
understandings were being carried into actual situations. Unfortunately, some teachers may not worry too much about
changes in a child's behavior beyond what can be accomplished
on a written test.

Some Principles of Learning Applied to Active Play

There are various basic facts about the nature of human
beings of which modern educators are more aware than educators of the past. Essentially, these facts involve some of the
fundamental aspects of the learning process, which all good
teaching should take into account. Older ideas of teaching
methods were based on the notion that the teacher was the sole
authority in terms of what was best for children, and that
children were expected to learn regardless of the conditions
surrounding the learning situation. For the most part, modern
teaching replaces the older concepts with methods that are
based on certain beliefs of educational psychology. Outgrowths
of these beliefs emerge in the form of *principles of learning*.
The following principles should provide important guidelines
for parents for arranging learning experiences for children, and
they suggest how desirable learning can take place when the
principles are satisfactorily applied to learning through active
play.
1. *The child's own purposeful goals should guide his learning
activities.*

For a desirable learning situation to prevail, parents should
consider certain features about purposeful goals that guide

learning activities. Of utmost importance is that the goal must seem worthwhile to the child. This will involve such factors as interest, attention, and motivation. Fortunately, in the recommended activities in this book involving active play, interest, attention, and motivation are "built-in" qualities. Thus, the parent does not necessarily need to "arouse" the child with various kinds of motivating devices such as "If you study your spelling I'll give you some money for candy."

2. *The child should be given sufficient freedom to create his own responses in the situation he faces.*

This principle indicates that *problem solving* is a very important way of human learning and that the child will learn mainly only through experience, either direct or indirect. This implies that the parent should provide every opportunity for the child to use his own judgment in the various situations that arise in the active play experience.

3. *The child agrees to and acts upon the learnings that he considers of most value to him.*

Children accept as most valuable those things which are of greatest interest to them. This principle implies in part, then, that there should be a satisfactory balance between *needs* and *interests* of children in their active play experiences. Although it is of extreme importance to consider the needs of children in developing experiences, the parent should keep in mind that their interest is needed if the most desirable learning is to take place.

4. *The child should be given the opportunity to share cooperatively in learning experiences with others under the guidance but not the control of the parent.*

This principle is concerned with those active play experiences that involve several players such as family members or other children. The point that should be emphasized here is that although learning is an individual matter, it can take place well in a group. This is to say that children learn individually but that socialization should be retained. This can be achieved even if there are only two members participating, the parent and the child.

5. *The parent should act as a guide who understands the child as a growing organism.*

This principle indicates that the parent should consider learning as an evolving process and not just as instant behavior. If the parent-tutor is to regard his or her teaching efforts in terms of guidance and direction of behavior that results in learning, wisdom must be displayed as to when to "step in and teach" and when to step aside and watch for further opportunities to guide and direct behavior. The application of this principle precludes an approach that is parent dominated. In this regard the parent-tutor could be guided by the old saying that "children should learn by monkeying and not by aping."

It is quite likely that parents will have good success in using the active play experiences recommended in this book if they attempt to apply the above principles. The main reason for this is that their efforts in helping their children learn through active play will be in line with those conditions under which learning takes place most effectively.

Chapter Three

WHY YOUR CHILD CAN LEARN THROUGH ACTIVE PLAY

ALTHOUGH we have mentioned the term *active play* numerous times, we have not yet explained what we mean by it. The reason for this is that we felt it would be more appropriate to do so at the outset of the present chapter.

To give the reader an idea of the difficulty in defining the word *play*, the 1972 edition of Webster's *New World Dictionary* gives no less than fifty-nine definitions of the term. Perhaps the reason for this is that the word *play* is used in so many different ways. This tends to require that authors who write about the subject of play give their own operational definition of it.

Our description of active play is *any enjoyable active interaction with one or more persons and/or natural forces.* Let us explain. This description places emphasis on *active* play as opposed to that which is more *passive* in nature. The kind of play we are concerned with is that which involves a total or near total *physical* response on the part of the child as he or she interacts with others and/or natural forces. When we use the term *natural forces* we are concerned primarily with the child playing by himself and not interacting with one or more persons. For example, if the child is trying to bounce a ball against a wall back and forth to himself, he is competing with such natural forces as gravity and air resistance. Of course, he could also be interacting with natural forces when playing with others.

Over a period of many years various theories of play have been advanced by psychologists and others in their study of human behavior. In general, these theories can be classified as the *classical* and *dynamic* theories. The classical theories attempt to explain *why* people play while the dynamic theories are more concerned with the *processes* of play. It is interesting to note that one of the recent dynamic theories conceives of play as being caused by the normal processes that produce learning. The present authors subscribe wholeheartedly to this learning theory, and subsequent discussion in the chapter will focus upon this particular aspect of play.

THE THEORY OF CHILD LEARNING
THROUGH ACTIVE PLAY

One of our main reasons for going into a rather detailed discussion of the theory of child learning through active play is based on the idea that some people tend to be skeptical about this approach to learning. Perhaps the reason for this is that so many individuals tend to associate learning only with work. They seem to feel that a child can learn only when "bent over a book." We hope that the following discussions will help to dispel this notion.

The active play approach to learning is concerned with how children can develop skills and concepts in the basic areas of reading, mathematics, and writing while actively engaged in such active play experiences as active games, stunts, and creative activities. It is based in part on the theory that children, being predominantly movement oriented, will learn better when what might be arbitrarily called *academic* learning takes place through pleasurable physical activity: that is, when the *motor* component (active play) operates at a maximal level in skill and concept development in school subjects that have been essentially oriented to *verbal* learning. This is not to say that active play learning and verbal learning are two mutually exclusive kinds of learning. It is recognized that in verbal learning, which involves almost complete abstract symbolic manipulations, there may be, among others, such motor components as tension, subvocal speech, and physiological changes in metabolism, which operate at a minimal level. It is also recognized that in active play where the learning is predominantly motor in nature, verbal learning is evident, although perhaps at a minimal level. For example, when a parent tutors a child through the active play medium there is a certain amount of verbalization (talking) in developing a "muscle sense" concept of the particular active play experience that is to be used.

The procedure of learning through active play involves the selection of an activity such as an active game, stunt, or creative activity, which is taught to the child and used as a learning activity for the development of a skill or concept in a specific subject area. An attempt is made to arrange an active learning situation so that a fundamental intellectual skill or concept is practiced or rehearsed in the course of participating in the active play experience.

In the following four chapters of the book a large number of such experiences are recommended for use by parents. However, it seems appropriate to give an example of such an experience at this point. The example that will be used for this purpose is a creative activity that we will call "Move Like Animals." (Animal imitations are very interesting activities for young children.) The parent can begin by reading the following to the child.

> We try to move like animals. We move like a bear. We move like an elephant. We move like a frog. We will try to move like these three animals. We will take five steps like a bear. We will take four steps like an elephant. We will take two jumps like a frog. Now we will do it the other way. Two jumps like a frog. Four steps like an elephant. Five steps like a bear.

The child proceeds by creating the various animal walks under the guidance of the parent. The following *mathematics skills and concepts* are built-in ingredients of this activity:

1. Rational counting. This means calling numbers in sequence — 1, 2, 3, etc.
2. Cardinal number ideas. Cardinal numbers are used in simple counting, and they indicate how many elements there are in a given assemblage — 1, 5, 15, etc. (*Ordinal* numbers are used to show order or succession — 1st, 2nd, 3rd, etc.)
3. Addition.
4. Commutative law. This means that the same total is arrived at regardless of the order in which the numbers are arranged: 2 plus 4 equals 6, and 4 plus 2 equals 6.

Following are some suggestions that a parent might consider in using the preceding active play experience. The parent should be sure to take into account the ability level of the child.

1. The child can count the animal movements as he makes them. Also he can add with the help of the parent to find how many movements there were altogether.
2. To use the cardinal number idea, after the child has taken five steps like a bear, the parent can ask, "How many steps did you take?"
3. To reinforce the understanding of commutative law the parent can put 5 + 4 + 2 and 2 + 4 + 5 on cards for the child to see before and/or after the activity.

The above suggestions do not include all of the possibilities that can be used with this sample activity, and the creative parent will obviously think of numerous others.

FACTORS THAT MAKE LEARNING EASIER THROUGH ACTIVE PLAY

During the early school years, and at ages six to eight particularly, it is likely that learning is frequently limited by a relatively short attention span rather than only by intellectual capabilities. Moreover, some children who do not appear to learn well in abstract terms can more readily grasp concepts when given an opportunity to use them in an applied manner. Since the child is a creature of movement, and also since he is likely to deal better in concrete rather than abstract terms, it would seem to follow naturally that the active play learning medium is well suited for him.

The preceding statement should not be interpreted to mean that the authors are suggesting that learning through active play experiences (motor learning) and passive learning experiences (verbal learning) are two different kinds of learning. The position is taken here that *learning is learning*, even though in the active play approach the motor component may be operating at a higher level than in most of the traditional types of learning activities.

The theory of learning accepted here is that learning takes place in terms of reorganization of the systems of perception (such as seeing and hearing) into a functional and integrated whole because of the result of certain stimuli. This implies, as mentioned in the preceding chapter, that *problem solving* is a very desirable and worthwhile way of human learning. In an active play situation that is well planned by the parent, a great deal of consideration should be given to the built-in possibilities for learning in terms of problem solving.

Another very important factor to consider with respect to the active play learning medium is that a considerable part of the learning of young children is motor in character, with the child devoting a good proportion of his attention to skills of a movement nature. Furthermore, learnings of a movement nature tend to use up a large amount of the young child's time and energy and are often associated with other learnings. In addition, it is well known by experienced classroom teachers at the primary level that the child's motor mechanism is active to the extent that it is almost an impossibility for him to remain for a very long period in a quiet state. To demand prolonged sedentary states of children is actually, in a sense, in defiance of a basic physiological principle. This is concerned with the child's basic metabolism, which was discussed in detail in the preceding chapter.

The comments made thus far have been concerned with some of the *general* aspects of the value of the active play learning medium. The following discussions will focus more *specifically* on certain factors in the active play learning medium that are very much in line with child learning. The factors are *motivation, muscle sense,* and *reinforcement,* all of which are somewhat interdependent and interrelated.

The Motivational Factor

Motivation can be thought of as something that causes a person to act. It is concerned with *why* people do certain things. What, how, when, and where a person does something is easy to determine. On the other hand, *why* one acts in a certain way is not so easy to observe. Thought of in these terms, motivation could be considered as something that gives direction to one's behavior.

For purposes of this discussion we should take into account

what we will arbitrarily call *outside* and *inside* motivation. Outside motivation can be described as applying incentives that are external to a given activity so that performance may be improved. Inside motivation means that a given activity is exciting enough for a person to engage in it for the purpose of enjoyment derived from the activity itself.

Outside motivation has been and continues to be used as a means of spurring individuals to achievement. This most often takes the form of various kinds of reward incentives. The main objection to this type of motivation is that it may tend to focus the learner's attention upon the reward rather than the learning task and the total learning situation.

People are motivated for different reasons. In general, the child is motivated when he discovers what seems to him to be a suitable reason for engaging in a certain activity. The most valid reason, of course, is that he sees a purpose for the activity and derives enjoyment from it. The child must feel that what he is doing is important and purposeful. When this occurs and the child gets the impression that he is being successful in a given situation, the motivation is within the activity (inside motivation). It comes about naturally as a result of the child's interest in the activity. It is the premise here that active play learning contains this built-in ingredient so necessary to desirable and worthwhile learning.

The following discussions of this section of the chapter will be concerned with three aspects of motivation that are considered to be an important part of the active play learning medium. These are (1) motivation in relation to *interest,* (2) motivation in relation to *knowledge of results,* and (3) motivation in relation to *competition.*

Motivation in Relation to Interest

It is important to have an understanding of the meaning of interest as well as an appreciation of how interests function as an aid to learning. Described simply, *interest* is a state of being, a way of reacting to a certain situation. *Interests* are those areas to which a child reacts with interest over an extended period of time.

It was stated in the last chapter (as a principle of learning) that a good condition for learning is a situation in which a child agrees with and acts upon the learnings that he considers of most value to him. This means that the child accepts as most valuable those things which are of greatest interest to him. To the very large majority of children, active play experiences are likely to be of the greatest *personal* value.

Under most circumstances a very high interest level is maintained in active play experiences simply because of the expectation of pleasure that children tend to associate with such activities. The structure of a learning activity is directly related to the length of time the learning act can be tolerated by the learner without loss of interest. Active play experiences by their very nature are more likely to be so structured than are many of the traditional learning activities.

Motivation in Relation to Knowledge of Results

Knowledge of results is also commonly referred to as *feedback*. It has been recognized for years that feedback is the process of providing the learner with information as to how accurate his reactions were. Psychologists usually refer to feedback as knowledge of various kinds that the performer received about his performance.

Many learning theorists agree that knowledge of results is the strongest, most important aspect controlling performance and learning and, further, that studies have repeatedly shown that there is no improvement without it, progressive improvement with it, and deterioration after its withdrawl. In fact, there appears to be a sufficient abundance of objective evidence that indicates that learning is usually more effective when one receives some immediate information on how he is progressing. It would appear rather obvious that such knowledge of results is an important aid to learning because one would have little idea of which of his responses were correct. Some psychologists compare it to trying to learn a task while blindfolded.

The active play learning medium provides almost instant knowledge of results because the child can actually *see* and *feel* himself involved in the activity. He does not become the victim of a poorly constructed paper-and-pencil test, the results of which may have little or no meaning for him.

Motivation in Relation to Competition

Modern society not only rewards *cooperation*, but also its direct opposite, *competition*. Since these forms of behavior are directly opposite, it is difficult to resolve a child's cooperative needs and his competitive needs. In a sense, one is confronted with a condition that, if not carefully handled, could place children in a state of conflict. Perhaps more often than not our cultural demands sanction the rewards of cooperation and competition without clear-cut standards with regard to specific conditions under which these forms of behavior might well be practiced. Thus, the child could be placed in somewhat of a quandary as to when to compete and when to cooperate.

In generalizing on the basis of the available evidence with regard to the subject of competition, it seems important to formulate the following concepts as guidelines for parents:

1. Very young children in general are not very competitive but become more so as they grow older.
2. There is a wide variety of competitive behavior among children: some are violently competitive while others are mildly competitive, and still others are not competitive at all.
3. Boys tend to be more competitive than girls.
4. Competition should be adjusted so that a child is more often a winner than a loser.
5. Competition and rivalry produce results in effort and speed of accomplishment.

In the active play experiences provided in this book, parents might well be guided by the above concepts. As far as the competitive aspects of certain active play experiences are concerned, they not only appear to be a good medium for learning because of the inside motivation, but this medium of learning can also provide for competitive needs of children in a pleasurable and enjoyable way.

The Muscle Sense Factor

Earlier in this chapter it was stated that the theory of learning accepted here is that learning takes place in terms of reorganization of the systems of perception into a functional and integrated whole as a result of certain stimuli. These systems of perception, or sensory processes as they are sometimes referred to, are ordinarily considered to consist of the senses of sight, hearing, touch, smell, and taste. Even though this point of view is convenient for most purposes, it no doubt greatly simplifies the ways by which information can be fed into the human organism. A number of sources of sensory input are overlooked, particularly the senses that enable the body to maintain its correct posture. In fact, the 60 to 70 pounds of muscle, which include over 600 in number, that are attached to the skeleton of the averaged-sized man could well be his most important sense organ.

Various estimates indicate that the visual sense brings us more than three-fourths of our knowledge. Therefore, it could be said with little reservation that man is *eye-minded*. However, one prominent physiologist, the late Dr. Arthur Steinhaus, has reported that a larger portion of the nervous system is devoted to receiving and integrating sensory input originating in the muscles and joint structures than is devoted to the eye and ear combined. In view of this it could also be contended that man is *muscle sense* minded.

The scientific term for muscle sense is *proprioception*. At the risk of becoming too technical, we nevertheless should mention that the *proprioceptors* are are sensory nerve terminals that give information concerning movements and position of the body. A proprioceptive feedback mechanism is involved, which in a sense regulates movement. Since children are so movement oriented, it appears a reasonable speculation that proprioceptive feedback from the receptors of muscles, skin, and joints may contribute to learning when active play is used to develop skills in reading, mathematics, and writing.

The Reinforcement Factor

In considering the relationship of active play learning to reenforcement theory, the meaning of reinforcement needs to be taken into account. An acceptable general description of reinforcement is that there is an increase in the efficiency of a response to a stimulus brought about by the concurrent action of another stimulus. A simple example of this would be when the parent gives praise and encouragement when the child is engaged in a task. Generally, the same principle applies when athletes refer to the "home court advantage," i.e. the home fans are present to spur them on. The basis for contending that active play learning is consistent with general reinforcement theory is that it reinforces attention to the learning task and learning behavior. It keeps the child involved in the learning activity, which is perhaps the major application for reinforcement procedures. Moreover, there is perhaps little in the way of human behavior that is not reinforced, or at least reinforcible, by feedback of some sort. The importance of muscle sense (proprioceptive) feedback has already been discussed in this particular regard.

In summarizing this discussion it would appear that active play learning generally establishes a more effective situation for learning for the following reasons:

1. The greater motivation of the child in the active play learning situation involves emphasis on those behaviors directly concerned with the learning activities.
2. The muscle sense emphasis in active play learning involves a greater number of *responses* associated with and conditioned to learning stimuli.
3. The gratifying aspects of active play learning provide a generalized situation of *reinforcers* for learning.

EVIDENCE TO SUPPORT THE THEORY

Any approach to learning should be based at least to some degree upon objective evidence produced by experimental research, and this is the subject of the following discussion.

There are a number of acceptable ways of studying how behavioral changes take place in children. In this regard, over a period of several years we have conducted numerous controlled studies concerned with the active play approach to learning. Our findings are suggestive enough to give rise to some interesting conclusions, which may be briefly summarized as follows:

1. In general, children tend to learn certain skills in reading, mathematics, and writing better through the active play learning medium than through many of the traditional approaches.
2. The active play approach, while favorable for both boys and girls, appears to be more favorable for boys.
3. When *active* play learning experiences are compared to *passive* play learning experiences (such as card games and board games), the active play approach is shown to be more favorable for both boys and girls.
4. The active play approach appears to be more favorable for children with average and below average intelligence.
5. For children with higher levels of intelligence, it may be possible to introduce more advanced concepts at an earlier age through the active play learning medium.

In addition to the above scientific findings, the many actual successful experiences with the active play learning activities recommended in this book should encourage parents to use the approach in an effort to help their children learn through pleasurable and enjoyable experiences.

Chapter Four

HOW TO IMPROVE YOUR CHILD'S ABILITY TO LEARN THROUGH ACTIVE PLAY

Hon does a parent go about improving a child's *ability to learn?* In the first place, something needs to be known about those abilities that need to be improved for desirable and worthwhile learning to take place. Generally speaking, these abilities can be classified under the broad area of *perceptual-motor* abilities. To understand the meaning of perceptual-motor we first need to define the terms *perception* and *motor* separately, and then derive a meaning when these two terms are combined.

Perception is concerned with how we obtain information through the senses and what we make of it. For purposes here, the term *motor* is concerned with the impulse of motion, resulting in a change of position through the various forms of body movement. When the two terms are put together (perceptual-motor), the implication is an organization of the information received through one or more of the senses, with related voluntary motor responses.

The development of perceptual-motor abilities in children is referred to by some child development specialists as the process of providing "learning-to-learn" activities. This means improvement upon such perceptual-motor qualities as body awareness, laterality and sense of direction, auditory and visual perception skills, and kinesthetic and tactile perception skills. A deficiency in one or more of these can detract from a child's ability to learn.

It is the function of this chapter to help parents determine if such deficiencies exist, along with recommended active play experiences to help improve upon them. Even though a deficiency does not exist in any of these factors, the active play experiences suggested can still be used to sharpen and improve upon these skills, which are so important to learning.

IMPROVING BODY AWARENESS THROUGH ACTIVE PLAY

As far as this subject is concerned, there are a number of terms that have been used by different writers to convey essentially the same meaning. Among others, these include body awareness, body schema, body image, body concept, body sense, and body experience. Regardless of which term is used, they all are likely to be concerned with the ability of the child to distinguish the particular features of the body parts. The present authors prefer to use the term *body-awareness* for this purpose.

Most child development specialists tend to agree that a child's knowledge of the names and function of the various body parts is a very important factor in the improvement of learning ability. For example, body-awareness gives a child a better understanding of the space his body takes and the relationship of its parts. Incidentally, these are critical factors in building foundations of mathematics competency.

It is doubtful that there are any absolutely foolproof methods of detecting problems of body-awareness in children. The reason for this is that many things that are said to indicate body-awareness problems can also be symptoms of other deficiencies. Nevertheless, parents should be alert to detect certain possible deficiencies.

Generally speaking, there are two ways in which deficiencies concerned with body-awareness might be detected. First, some deficiencies can be noticed, at least in part, by observing certain behaviors; second, there are some relatively simple diagnostic techniques that can be used to detect such deficiencies. The following generalized list contains examples of both of these possibilities and is presented to assist the parent in this particular regard:

1. One technique often used to diagnose possible problems of body-awareness is to have children make a drawing of themselves. The main reason for this is to see if certain parts of the body are not included in the drawing. Since the child's interest in drawing a man dates from his earliest attempts to represent things symbolically, it is possible, through typical

drawings of young children, to trace certain characteristic stages of perceptual development. It has also been found that the procedure of drawing a picture of himself assists in helping to detect if there is lack of body-awareness.

2. Sometimes the child with a lack of body-awareness may show tenseness in his movements. At the same time he may be unsure of his movements as he attempts to move the body segments (arm or leg).

3. If the child is instructed to move a body part such as placing one foot forward, he may direct his attention to the body part before making the movement; or, he may look at another child to observe the movement before he attempts to make the movement himself. (This could also be because of not understanding the instructions for the movement)

4. When instructed to use one body part (arm) he may move the corresponding body part (other arm) when it is not necessary. For example, he may be asked to swing the right arm and may also start to swing the left arm at the same time.

5. In such activities as catching an object, the child may turn toward the object when it is not necessary. For example, when a beanbag thrown to him approaches close to the child, he may move forward with either side of the body rather than trying to catch the beanbag with his hands while both feet remain stationary.

ACTIVE PLAY EXPERIENCES
INVOLVING BODY-AWARENESS

In general, it might be said that when a child is given the opportunity to use his body freely in active play experiences, an increase in body-awareness occurs. More specifically, there are certain activities that can be useful in helping children identify and understand the use of various body parts as well as the relationship of these parts. Over a period of time we have conducted a number of experiments to determine the effect of participating in certain active play experiences on body-awareness. The following activities have proved to very useful for this purpose.

Busy Bee

The parent and child stand facing each other. To begin with, the parent can be the *caller*. The parent makes calls such as "shoulder-to-shoulder," "toe-to-toe," or "hand-to-hand." As the calls are made, the parent and child go through the motions with each other. After a few calls, the parent calls out "Busy Bee!" and the two of them, the parent and the child, run to a point that was previously decided on. The idea is to see who can reach this point first. The activity continues with the child being the caller. When this activity is used with a group of players, the caller stands in the middle of the activity area and makes the calls. At the signal of "Busy Bee" all players try to find a new partner, and the caller also tries to find a partner. The player who does not find a partner is the caller when the activity is played again.

To give the reader an idea of how such a play activity can improve upon body-awareness, we report here on an experiment using this particular activity with a group of several kindergarten children. Before the activity, the children were asked to draw a picture of themselves. Many did not know how to begin, and others omitted some of the major limbs in their drawings. After playing Busy Bee, the children were asked again to draw a picture of themselves. This time they were more successful. All of the drawings had bodies, heads, arms, and legs. Some of them had hands, feet, eyes, and ears. A few even had teeth and hair.

Mirrors

To start this activity, the parent can be the leader and stands facing the child a short distance away. The parent goes through a variety of movements and the child tries to do exactly the same thing, that is, he acts as a mirror. The child and parent take turns being the leader. This can be done with several players by having them stand in line with the leader in front of them and going through the different movements.

In this activity the child becomes aware of different body parts and movements as the leader makes the various movements. The parent should be alert to see how quickly the child is able to do the movements that are made.

Move Along

The child lies on his back on the floor. The parent gives a signal such as a clap of the hands, and the child moves his arms and legs in any way that he chooses. The parent then gives the name of a movement such as "Move your legs like a bicycle," and then gives the signal to begin the movement. This same activity can be used with several players.

The parent should observe closely to see how rapidly the child responds to the movements called. Also, if the activity is used with several players, the parent should observe to see if the child or other children are waiting to see what others are going to do before making the correct movement.

Body Tag

To start this game the child is *It*. He chases the parent and attempts to tag him/her. If he is successful the parent becomes *It*. To be officially tagged, a specific part of the body must be tagged by *It*. Thus, the activity could be shoulder tag, arm tag, or leg tag as desired. This activity can be played with several players and is actually much more fun when there are more than two players.

The parent observes the child to see whether or not he tags the correct body part. To add more interest to the activity, the one who is *It* can call out the body part to be tagged during each session of the activity.

Measuring Worm

The child extends his body along the floor in a straight line facing down. His weight is supported by his hands and toes. With arms and legs extended he takes very short steps until his feet are near his hands. He then moves ahead on his hands with very short "steps" until his body is extended again. He continues to do this for a specified distance.

It should be brought to the attention of the child how he is using his hands and feet to move along like a measuring worm. In discussing this activity with the child, the use of the body parts, hands, arms, feet, and legs is mentioned. During the activity the parent can see how the child reacts to the directions. Sometimes children confuse hands and arms and feet and legs.

Squat Through

From a standing position the child assumes a squatting stance, placing the hands on the surface area to the outside of his legs with the palms flat and the fingers forward. This is count number 1. Switching the weight to the hands and arms, the child extends his legs sharply to the rear until the body is straight. The weight of the body is now on the hands and the balls of the feet. This is count number 2. On count number 3 the child returns to the squatting position, and on count number 4 the child returns to the erect standing position.

The child is able to see the function of certain body parts as the weight is shifted. After directions are given for the performance of the activity, the parent can notice how well they are followed with reference to the correct position of the body parts concerned.

Touch

In this activity the parent calls out body parts, which the child tries to touch with each other. Some calls could be "Touch your knee with your arm," "Touch your ankle with your hand." As can be seen, the possibilities are many. The parent can observe to see if the correct touches are made.

Run Under

A balloon or a beach ball can be used for this activity. The parent calls out a body part and throws the ball or balloon into the air. The child tries to run under the ball or balloon and have it touch the body part called out by the parent.

Everybody Goes

The child stands at one end of the activity area. The parent stands in the middle of the area facing the child. At the opposite end of the area there is a goal line. The activity is started with the following rhyme:

Head, shoulders, knees, and toes.
Eyes, ears, mouth, and nose.
Off and running everybody goes.

On the last word, "goes," the child tries to run to the other end without being tagged by the parent. The activity continues with the child and parent changing places. When several players are used they stand in a line at the end of the activity area, and the one selected to be *It* stands in the center. When they run to the goal line all of those tagged become helpers of *It* and play continues.

As the rhyme is recited the child (children) in the line does the following motions: head — place both hands on the head; shoulders — place both hands on the shoulders; knees — bend at the waist and place hands on knees; toes — bend on down and touch the toes and resume standing position; eyes — point to the eyes; mouth — point to the mouth; nose — point to the nose.

It is a good idea for the parent to recite the rhyme, as he/she can judge how fast this should be done. The more accomplished the child (children) becomes, the faster the rhyme can be recited, and the child or children can recite the rhyme in unison. When the activity is first used, the parent can observe how closely the child is reacting to what the rhyme says. It may be found that the child is having difficulty. Thus, the activity becomes a means of diagnosing a lack of body-awareness. It will be noted that with practice a child will improve in response to the rhyme. A different form of movement can be substituted for *running*: that is, it can be "Off and skipping (hopping, jumping, etc.) everybody goes."

Clap and Tap

Sometimes the activity can be presented to the child as follows:

I clap with my hands.
Clap, clap, clap.
I tap with my foot.
Tap, tap, tap.
I point my toe.
And around I go.
Clap, clap, clap.
Tap, tap, tap.

The parent can read this to the child, then during participation he/she can see how well the child follows the body movement directions.

Snowflakes

Creative activities are highly recommended on the basis that when a child is able to use his body freely, there is a strong likelihood that there will be increased body-awareness. This creative activity and those that follow are intended for this purpose. The parent reads to the child, and then with various degrees of parent guidance the child tries to depict the activity in the reading selection by creating his own responses.

Snow!
Snowflakes fall.
They fall down.
Down, down, down.
Around and around.
They fall to the ground.
Could you move like snowflakes?

Mr. Snowman and Mr. Sun

See Mr. Snowman.
See Mr. Sun.
Mr. Snowman sees Mr. Sun.
Mr. Snowman is going.
Going, going, going.
Mr. Snowman is gone.
Be Mr. Snowman.

Could you do like Mr. Snowman?

Tick, Tock

Listen to the clock.
It says "Tick, Tock" as it keeps the time.
Would you like to play you are a clock?
This is the way.
Stand up.
Hold your hands.
Keep your arms straight.
Now keep time with the clock by swinging your arms.
Ready.
Swing your arms from side to side.
Swing them to the tick tock of the clock.
Can you keep time as you move from side to side?

Automobile

Pretend you are an automobile.
Hum like the engine.
Hmm! Hmm! HMM!
Your feet are the wheels.
Go like an automobile.
Hum as you go.
Can you hum while you go like an automobile?

In these activities the parent can carefully observe the movements of the child with reference to the body parts used in the creative activities. "Did you use your arms? Your legs?" and so on. If the parent desires, a drum or suitable recording can be used as accompaniment.

IMPROVING LATERALITY AND DIRECTIONALITY THROUGH ACTIVE PLAY

The terms *laterality* and *directionality* are probably new to many parents. These qualities are concerned with distinction of the body sides and sense of direction. More specifically, laterality is an internal awareness of the left and right sides of the body in relation to the child himself. It is concerned with the child's knowledge of how each side of the body is used separately or together. Directionality is the projection into space of laterality: that is, the awareness of left and right, up and down, over and under, etc., in the world around the child. Stated in another way, directionality in space is the ability to project outside the body the laterality that the child has developed within himself.

The categories of laterality and directionality make up the broader classification of *directional awareness*. The development of this quality is most important in that it is an essential element for reading and writing. These two basic R's require the hand and/or eyes to move from the left to the right in a coordinated manner. Also, interpretation of left and right directions is an important requirement for the child in dealing with the environment. It is interesting to note that some children who have *not* developed laterality quite often will write numbers sequentially from left to right. However, when doing addition or subtraction, they may want to start from the left instead of the right. Active play activities designed to differentiate right and left sides of the body are an important part of remedial arithmetic.

Since laterality and directionality are important aspects of body-awareness, some of the methods of detecting deficiencies in body-awareness mentioned earlier in the chapter also apply here. In addition, it may be noted that the child is inclined to use just the dominant side of his body. Also, confusion may result if the child is given directions for body movements that call for a specific direction in which he is to move. In activities that require a child to run to a given point, such as a base, he may tend to veer away from it. Or, he may not perceive the position of other children in a game and, as a consequence may run into them frequently. These are factors that parents can observe in children in their natural play environment, or in their movements about the home.

Some specialists have indicated that they have had success with a specific test of laterality. This test is given on a 4-inch wide walking board that is 2 feet in length. The child tries to walk forward, backward, and sideways, right to left and left to right, while attempting to maintain his balance. It is suggested that a child with a laterality problem will experience difficulty moving one of the ways sideward, ordinarily from left to right.

ACTIVE PLAY EXPERIENCES INVOLVING
LATERALITY AND DIRECTIONALITY

Generally speaking, a relatively large number of active play experiences involve some aspects of lateralness, while a more moderate number are concerned with directionality. Some active play experiences involve *unilateral* movements, those performed with one side or part of the body. Many active play experiences provide for *bilateral* movement. This means that both sides or segments of the body are in action at the same time in the same manner, as in catching a large ball with both hands. *Cross-lateral* movement is involved when segments of the body are used at the same time but in a different manner. In fielding a ground ball a child may catch it in one hand and trap it with the other. Many active play experiences are concerned with changing direction, which is likely to involve directionality. The active play experiences that follow have been selected because they contain certain experiences in laterality and/or directionality. Also, in some of the activities, these experiences are more pronounced and receive more emphasis than might be the case with certain other activities.

Zig Zag Run

With the individual child the parent can set up various objects about 4 feet apart and have the child run around them, first to the left and then to the right and so on. This activity gives practice in changing directions as the child runs around the objects. The parent can closely observe how much difficulty is encountered in performing the task. With several players, children can be put into two teams and the activity carried out in relay fashion.

Hit It

The parent and the child stand a short distance apart. The

parent tosses an object such as a balloon or beachball to the child. The idea is for the child to try to hit the object in the direction called out by the parent. If the parent calls out "left" the child tries to hit it to the left. If the parent calls out "down" the child tries to hit it downward. The parent can call out any direction desired. After a time the parent and child can change with the child throwing the ball to the parent and going through the same procedure.

Move Around

The parent and the child stand a short distance apart. The parent calls out directions in which the child is to move, such as "move to the right," "move forward," "move backward," and so on. After a time the parent and child change positions and the child becomes the caller.

Catch the Cane

The parent stands a short distance away from the child and, with one finger, holds a stick (cane) upright. When the parent calls "Go" the cane is let go and is allowed to fall. The child tries to catch the cane before it drops to the surface area. Then the parent and child change places. This activity helps in the development of directionality, eye-hand coordination, and listening discrimination.

Ostrich Tag

The child and parent stand a short distance apart. To start with, the parent is *It*. The parent tries to tag the child as the child tries to avoid being tagged. The child can protect himself by standing in ostrich fashion: that is, he may stand on one foot with his hands behind his back. The other leg is swung back and forth to help maintain balance. If the parent tags the child before he is in position or after he has moved, the child becomes *It*. It can be more fun if there are several players in this activity.

Before the activity starts the parent can indicate to the child on which foot he is to stand. The parent can then take note if he is standing on the designated foot. The parent might also take note if the child is having difficulty in maintaining balance when standing on one foot.

Crab Walk

The child sits on the surface area with his knees bent and his hands on the surface area behind his hips. He raises his hips until his trunk is straight. In this position he walks forward and backward or to the side on his hands and feet.

The number of steps taken may be specified with reference to direction, i.e. so many steps forward and so many backward. Also, the parent can call out the directions for the "crab" to pursue: forward, backward, or sideward left or right.

Up and Down

The child and parent stand facing each other holding hands. The child stoops down. When he stands the parent stoops down. They continue doing this. They can go up and down any number of times, calling out whether they are up or down.

Rocking Chair

The child and parent sit on the surface area facing each other, with feet close to the body. Each can sit on the feet of the other or very close together. They grasp each other just above the elbows in this position, and rock back and forth. They call out the words "forward" and "back" as they rock.

Log Roll

The child assumes a position on his stomach on a soft surface such as a thick rug. He extends his body by placing his arms over the head along the surface area. The arms are straight. The legs are also extended with the feet together and the toes pointed. The child then uses his head, shoulders, and hips to turn 360 degrees along the surface area. The child should attempt to roll in a straight line in either direction down the surface area. This is a good activity for developing directional movement. The parent should observe if the child is rolling in a straight line. This can be improved by keeping the body extended and straight. The child can call out his movements as he rolls first to one side and then to the other.

Go and Stop

This activity requires at least three players. They stand around the activity area with one person designated as the leader. The leader points in a given direction and says "Hop that way." Or the leader may say "Skip to the wall." When the leader calls out "Stop," all of the players must stoop down. The idea is not to be the last one down. The last person down has a point scored against him, and the activity continues for a specified amount of time.

In the early stages of this activity, it is a good idea for the parent to be the leader so he/she can control the various calls. The parent can observe if a child is unable to go immediately in the direction the leader specifies. The parent should be alert to see if a child watches another before making a movement. This can suggest whether a child is having difficulty in following directions.

Over and Under Relay

This activity requires several players, family members and/or other children. The players form two or more rows with an equal number in each row. The first player in each row is given a ball or other object that can be passed to the players behind. At a signal the first player hands the object over his head to the second player; the second player passes it back between his legs to the third player; the third player passes it back over his head, etc. When the last player receives the object, he runs to the head of his row and the same procedure is followed. This procedure continues until the first player returns to the head of his row. The row first completing the circuit is the winner.

This activity gives children an opportunity to pass an object in a backward direction while at the same time changing direction. The parent can have the players call out "over" and "under" as the case may be so that they can become familiar with the meaning. The terminology can be changed to *up* and *down* if the parent desires. (Any active play experience that helps a child understand terms such as these can also help him in arithmetic because these terms are critical to arithmetic competency.)

Corn Race

This activity, which requires several players, is a modern version of a game that goes back into the history of our country. In early times while adults were husking corn, the children played games with the ears of corn. The players are divided into two or more rows. In front of each row a circle about 3 feet in diameter is made on the playing area to represent a corn basket. Straight ahead beyond each of the corn baskets, four smaller circles are made about 10 feet apart. In each of the four small circles is places an object (a block, beanbag, etc.) representing an ear of corn. At a signal, the first person in each row runs to the small circles in front of and in line with his row, picks up the corn one ear at a time, and puts all the ears in the corn basket. The second person takes the ears from the corn basket and replaces them in the small circles, and the activity proceeds until all members have run and returned to their places.

This activity provides an opportunity to move forward and backward and to place objects in the process. The parent should take note if a child is confused about the particular task. Assistance can be given if the child needs it.

Change Circle Relay

This activity requires several players. The players are arranged in two or more rows. Three circles are made side by side on the surface area a given distance in front of each row. In the circle to the left of each row, three objects are placed. These objects can be anything that can be made to stand upright, such as cardboard milk cartons. The first child runs to the circle and moves the objects to the next circle; the second child moves them to the last circle, and then each succeeding child repeats this process; the objects are moved from the first circle to the second circle to the third circle, and then back to the first circle. All of the objects must remain standing. If one falls, the last child to touch it must return and set it up. The activity is complete when all players in a row have had an opportunity to change the objects from one circle to another.

The number of objects can be varied, and the activity can be started with just one object. This activity gives children an opportunity to execute change in direction by placing objects in specified places. If the parent desires, the circles can be labeled with *left, center,* and *right.*

The Rhythm Game

Creative parents can develop their own rhythmic activities and use movements that they desire. The following original verse, which indicates movement to be made, is an example:

Point to the left.
Now point to the right.
Now turn around with all your might.
Take one step forward.
Take one step back.
Now try to be a jumping jack.
Point your arms out.
Point your toes in.
Now give yourself a little spin.
Now turn your head.
Now bend your knees.
Now buzz around like a hive of bees.

It is an interesting practice to have the child, with the guidance of the parent, also create experiences along the above lines. It has been our experience that activities of this nature are likely to be of extreme value because they are devised to meet the needs of a child or children in a specific situation.

IMPROVING THE FORMS OF PERCEPTION
THROUGH ACTIVE PLAY

At the beginning of this chapter we defined perception as how we obtain information through the senses and what we make of it. We should perhaps mention that this term is often defined differently by different sources. For example, one source describes perception as an individual's awareness of and reaction to stimuli. Another source refers to it as the process by which the individual maintains contact with his environment. Still another source describes it as the mental interpretation of messages received through the senses. While there are many descriptions of the term *perception,* it is likely that the reader will notice that these descriptions are more alike than they are different. Our description of perception tends to place the meaning of it in more or less simple terms.

According to learning theorist Dr. Jean Piaget, perception is developmental: it changes with age and experience. Development of perception occurs in three major periods: (1) sensorimotor intelligence, which occurs during the period from birth to about two years, is concerned with learning to coordinate various perceptions and movements; (2) the ages from two to about eleven or twelve involve preparation for and organization of concrete operations, and deal with the acquisition of language (it is during this period that the child learns to deal logically with his surroundings); and (3) the formal operations that occur after the age of eleven or twelve, and deal with the development of abstract and formal systems.

Learning theorists agree that the forms of perception most involved in learning are *auditory* perception, *visual* perception, *kinesthetic* perception, and *tactile* perception. These are the topics for discussion in the remainder of this chapter.

Auditory Perception

It was estimated several years ago that about 75 percent of the waking hours are spent in verbal communication — 45 percent in listening, 30 percent in speaking, 16 percent in reading, and the remaining 9 percent in writing. If this estimate is true, the importance of developing skills of listening cannot be denied. If children are going to learn effectively, care should be taken to improve upon their auditory perception — *the mental interpretation of what a person hears.* Without question, selective attention to sound is essential in helping children increase their effective use of auditory information. Moreover, by becoming a better listener and learning to ignore unrelated noise, the child can begin to hear important concepts needed to improve academic performance.

Before getting into some of the specific active play experiences involving auditory perception, it might be a good idea to discuss certain factors concerned with what we will call the *auditory input phase* that is used when presenting the activities recommended in this book. The factors that we will take into account are (1) preparing the child for listening, (2) parent-child verbal interaction, and (3) directionality of sound.

Preparing the Child for Listening

Since it is likely that explaining an active play activity will originate with the parent, care should be taken to prepare the child for listening. In preparing the child to listen, the parent should be aware that it is of extreme importance to take into consideration the comfort of the child, and that attempts should be made to hold his attention. Although evidence concerning the effect of environmental distraction on listening effectiveness is in short supply, there is reason to believe that distraction does interfere with listening comprehension.

These factors have a variety of implications for the auditory input phase of the active play teaching-learning situation. For example, it might be wise for the parent to consider that an object, such as a ball, could become a distraction when an activity is being explained. The attention of the child is sometimes focused on the ball, and he may not listen to what is being said. The parent might wish to conceal such an object until time for its use is most appropriate.

Parent-Child Verbal Interaction

Since the auditory input phase should be a two-way process between the parent and the child, it is important to take into account certain factors involving verbal interaction of the child with the parent. An important function in the parent-child verbal interaction is that which is concerned with the time given for questions after the parent has given an explanation. The parent should give time for questions from the child but should be very skillful in the use of such questions. It must be determined immediately whether or not a question is a legitimate one. This implies that the type of questions asked can help the parent determine how well he or she did in explaining the activity. For example, if numerous questions are asked, it is apparent that either the explanation of the parent was incomplete or the child was not paying attention.

Directionality of Sound

Previously when we discussed directionality, we were concerned with directionality in space. Here we are concerned with directionality of sound, or the direction from which a sound comes. It has been found that as far as directionality of sound is concerned, children will make their first movement in the direction from which a sound comes. For example, if a given verbal cue instructs a child to move his body or a body segment to the left, but the cue comes from the right side, the child's initial movement response is very likely to be to the right, followed by a reverse response to the left. This means that when we deal with young children in terms of the directions of movement responses, we should make certain that sound cues come from the direction in which the movement responses are to be made. This means that if we are going to say "move left," we should stand a little to the left of the child. Some children may have enough difficulty determining right from left without our further confounding them.

Active Play Experiences Involving Auditory Perception

Red Rover

The child stands at one end of the activity area, and the parent stands in the middle of the activity area. The area can be about 20 to 30 feet long and about 15 to 20 feet wide. The parent calls "Red Rover, Red Rover let (name of child) come over." The child tries to run to the other end of the playing area before being tagged by the parent. The parent and child change places so that the child can have a turn at being the caller. The child must listen carefully and run at exactly the right time. This activity can be used with several players if desired.

Red Light

The parent and child take positions the same as for Red Rover, except that the parent has his or her back to the child. The parent calls out "Green light." At that signal the child starts to run to the other end of the playing area. At any time the parent can call out "Red light," and turn around to face the child. If the child is caught moving he must go back to the starting line. If not, the parent calls "Green light" again and the activity continues in this manner. The idea is for the child to get all the way to the goal line on the opposite end of the activity area. The child and parent should change places frequently so that the child can be the caller. The child must listen closely so as not to get caught moving when "Red light" is called.

Clap and Move

The parent claps his or her hands using slow beats or fast beats. The child moves around the area to the sound of the hand claps. The child walks on the slow beat and runs on the fast beat. The child must be alert to respond to the different beats. After a while the parent and child can exchange places.

Freeze and Melt

The child moves around the activity area in any way he chooses, such as walking, running, or hopping. When the parent calls out "Freeze," the child must stop. When the word "Melt" is called out, the child begins to move around again. The child must listen very closely so as not to be caught moving when the word "Freeze" is called. After a time the parent and child can change places, with the child doing the calling.

Boiling Water

The child stands a short distance away from the parent, holding a rubber ball. When the parent calls "Cold water," the child passes the ball to the parent. If the parent calls "Warm water," the child rolls the ball to the parent. If the parent calls "Boiling water," the child throws the ball into the air. The parent and child should change places frequently so that the child can be the caller. This activity can be used as a diagnostic technique to determine how well the child can distinguish auditory cues and perform the action required.

Stoop Tag

The child runs around the activity, saying "I am happy! I am free! I am down! You can't catch me!" At the word "down," the child stoops down to avoid being tagged by the parent. If the child is tagged when not stooping, a point can be scored for the parent. The parent and child should change positions frequently.

The child first learns to act on the basis of verbal instruction by others. In this regard it has been suggested that later he learns to guide and direct his own behavior on the basis of his own language activities — he talks to himself, giving himself instructions. In fact, speech as a form of communication between children and parents later becomes a means of organizing the child's own behavior. The function that was previously divided between two people — the child and the parent — later becomes a function of human behavior. In this activity the child tells himself what to do and then does it. He says "I am down," then carries out this action.

Dog Chase

This activity requires four or more players. They are divided into two or more groups. The members of each group are given the name of a dog, such as collie, poodle, and so on. The small groups then mingle into one large group. The parent throws a ball or other object away from the groups, at the same time calling out one of the dog names. All of the players with this dog name run after the object. The one who gets possession of it first becomes the leader for the next time. The parent can use this activity as a diagnostic technique by observing if the child who is the "principal" player reacts slowly or does not react at all to the auditory input.

As will be seen in the following chapter, reading specialists are becoming more and more aware of the importance of auditory perception as one of the early steps in learning to read. It is suggested by some that the ability to discriminate sounds auditorily is not only an advantage in speech but probably gives an important boost in reading ability. It has been found that active play experiences can provide an important part in the aspect of auditory perception that is concerned with auditory discrimination.

Visual Perception

Visual perception can be defined as the *mental interpretation of what a person sees*. A number of aspects of visual perception have been identified, and children who have a deficiency in any of these may have difficulty in school performance.

Various estimates indicate that the visual sense brings us upwards of three-fourths of our knowledge. If this is true, then certainly important consideration should be given to how well active play experiences can contribute to visual perception.

Active Play Experiences Involving Visual Perception

The activities that follow are primarily concerned with *visualization* and *visual-motor coordination*. Visualization involves visual image, which is the mental reconstruction of visual experience, or the result of mentally combining a number of visual experiences. Visual-motor coordination is concerned with visual-motor tasks that involve the working together of vision and movement.

Hit the Balloon

The child is given a big balloon, and he tries to hit it as many times as he can with his hand before the balloon touches the ground. Other things that the child can do with the balloon are to hit it off a wall or hit the balloon back and forth with the parent. This activity is good for eye-hand coordination.

Big Ball, Little Ball

The parent and child sit on the floor about 10 feet from each other. One has a large ball such as a beach ball and the other has a smaller ball. The parent gives a signal, and the big ball is rolled and the small ball is thrown. Both the parent and the child try to catch the ball, and the activity continues in this manner.

Peas Porridge

The child and parent stand facing each other. They slap knees, clap their own hands and each other's hands while they say "Peas porridge hot, Peas porridge cold. Peas porridge in the pot. Nine days old!"

Ball Pass

This activity requires four or more players. The players are divided into two or more groups, and each group forms a small circle. The object is to pass a ball around the circle to see who can get it around first. The parent gives the directions for the ball to be passed or tossed from one player to another. For example, the parent may say "Pass the ball to the right, toss the ball over two players," and so on. The activity may be varied by using several balls of different sizes and weights. This activity provides a good opportunity to improve eye-hand coordination, and it has been observed that after practice in this activity, poor coordination is likely to be improved.

Policeman

The parent is the policeman and stands a given distance away from the child. The parent (policeman) carries a card, red on one side and green on the other. At the signal to go (green) from the parent the child sees how far he can go before the stop signal (red) is given. If the child moves after the stop signal is given, he must go back to the original starting point. The parent and child can change places frequently.

Rather than using the colors, the words *Stop* and *Go* can be used on the card so that the child can become familiar with the words as well as the colors. This activity helps the child coordinate movement with the visual experience. It can also help the child become more adept at visual-motor association. The parent should be alert to observe if the child does not stop on signal.

Keep It Up

Depending upon the ability level of the child, a large rubber ball, a beach ball, or a large balloon can be used for this activity. On a signal the child tosses the ball into the air, and together the parent and child see how long they can keep it up without its touching the surface area. This is a good activity for the improvement of eye-hand coordination.

Mother May I?

The child stands at one end of the activity area. The parent has cards showing object pairs, similar and different. (Together the parent and child can cut pictures from magazines and paste them on the cards.) The parent holds up one pair of the cards. If the paired objects or symbols are the same, the child may take one giant step forward. If the child moves when he sees an unpaired set of cards, he must return to the starting line. The object of the activity is to reach the finish line on the opposite side of the activity area. The parent may select cards to test any level of visual discrimination. Using pairs of cards for categorizing pictures would make use of concept and language development.

Ball Handling Activities

Various kinds of ball-handling activities provide outstanding experiences for eye-hand coordination. The activities that follow can be used for this purpose and are a great deal of fun to try. The type of ball used should be one that is suited to the ability level of the child.

STATIONARY BOUNCE. Using both hands, the child bounces the ball to the surface area and catches it while standing in place. This can be repeated any number of times.

WALKING BOUNCE. Using both hands, the child bounces the ball to the surface area and catches it while walking.

PARTNER BOUNCE. Using both hands, the child bounces the ball to the parent, who returns it. The distance between the parent and child can be increased as desired.

STATIONARY TAP. The child taps the ball with one hand while standing in place. Either hand can be used, depending upon the individual child, and the tapping can be repeated any number of times. (In bouncing, the child gains control of the ball each time; in tapping, the child keeps it going for a given number of times without gaining control of the ball.)

WALKING TAP. The child taps the ball with either hand while walking along. This can be done any number of times.

THROW AND CATCH. The child throws the ball into the air and catches it. The height of the throw can be increased if desired.

BOUNCE-CLAP-CATCH. The child bounces the ball to the surface area and claps the hands before catching it.

BOUNCE-TURN-CATCH. The child bounces the ball and turns around to catch it before it bounces a second time. At the onset of this activity it may be a good idea for the child to throw the ball into the air and then turn around and catch it on the bounce. In this variation the child has more time to turn around before the ball bounces.

LEG-OVER-BOUNCE. The child bounces the ball, swings a leg over it, and catches it. This can be done with either leg, and then legs can be alternated.

LEG-OVER-TAP. This is the same as the Leg-Over-Bounce except that the child causes the ball to bounce by continuous tapping.

Kinesthetic Perception

Kinesthesis, the kinesthetic sense, has been described in many ways. Some definitions of the term are somewhat comprehensive, while others are less so. One comprehensive description of kinesthesis is that it is the sense which enables us to determine the position of the segments of the body, their rate, extent, and direction of movement, the position of the entire body, and the characteristics of total body motion. Another, less complicated description of the term characterizes it as the sense that tells the individual where his body is and how it moves.

In summarizing the many definitions of the term *kinesthesis*, the following four factors seem to be constant, thus emphasizing the likenesses of the many definitions of the term: (1) position of the body segments, (2) precision of movement, (3) balance, and (4) space orientation. For our discussion here we will think of kinesthetic perception as the *mental interpretation of the sensation of body movement*.

Although there are a number of specific test items that are supposed to measure kinesthesis, the use of such tests may be of questionable value in diagnosing deficiencies in young children. Therefore, our recommendation is that parents resort to the observation of certain behaviors and mannerisms of children, using some simple diagnostic techniques to determine deficiencies in kinesthetic sensitivity.

Various authorities on the subject suggest that children with kinesthetic problems possess certain characteristics that may be identifying factors. For example, it has been indicated that a child who is deficient in kinesthetic sensitivity will likely be clumsy, awkward, and inefficient in his movements and impaired in getting acquainted with and handling the world of objects. A child who has difficulty in the use of his hands or his body in attempting to perform unfamiliar tasks involving body movement can no doubt benefit from activities involving kinesthesis.

With reference to the above, the parent should be on the alert to observe a child who has difficulty with motor coordination: that is, using the muscles in such a manner that they work together effectively. Such lack of coordination may be seen in children who have difficulty in performing the movement skills that involve an uneven rhythm, such as *skipping*. Parents can observe these deficiencies in the natural play activity of children, and a skill such as skipping can be used as a diagnostic technique in identifying such problems. (Skipping starts with a step and a hop on the same foot and can be taught from the walk. The push-off should be such a forceful upward one that the foot leaves the surface area. To maintain balance, a hop is taken. The sequence is step, push-off high, hop. The hop occurs on the same foot that was pushing off, and this is the skip. Some children will perform a variation of the skip around four years of age. With proper instruction, a majority of children should be able to accomplish this movement by age six.)

Since balance is an important aspect of kinesthesis, simple tests for balance can be administered to determine if there is a lack of proficiency. One such test would be to have the child stand on either foot. Ordinarily, a child should be able to maintain such a position for a period of at least five seconds.

Active Play Experiences Involving Kinesthetic Perception

Since kinesthetic sensitivity is concerned with the sensation of movement and orientation of the body in space, it is not an easy matter to isolate specific active play experiences suited *only* for this purpose. The reason for this, of course, is that practically all active play experiences involve total or near total physical response. Therefore, practically all active play experiences are of value in the improvement of kinesthetic sensitivity. However, the kinds of active play experiences that make the child particularly aware of the movement of certain muscle groups, as well as those where he encounters resistance, are of particular value in helping the child develop kinesthetic awareness of his body.

Rush and Pull

This activity requires a rope about 15 feet in length. The parent secures one end of the rope to an object. This object can be a chair or a bench and heavy enough to offer some resistance when the child pulls on the rope. The child should be able to pull the object, but at the same time it should not be too heavy for him to do so. The child stands a short distance away from the rope. On a signal from the parent, the child runs to the rope and tries to pull the object. A game can be made out of the activity by such things as seeing how long it takes to pull the object a certain distance or simply pulling the object over a predetermined line.

In this activity the child experiences resistance as he tries to pull the object. He also experiences the feel of the muscle groups of the arms and legs working together.

Poison

This activity requires several players. The players form a circle and join hands. A circle is drawn on the activity area inside the circle of players and about 12 to 18 inches in front of the feet of the circle of players. With hands joined, they pull and tug each other, trying to make one or more of the players step into the drawn circle. Anyone who steps into the circle is said to be "poisoned." As soon as a person is poisoned, someone calls out "Poison!" and the one who is poisoned becomes *It* and gives chase to the others. The other players run to various objects of certain material previously designated as *safety*, such as wood, stone, or metal. All of the players tagged are poisoned and become chasers. After those not tagged have reached safety, the leader calls out "Change!" and they must run to another safety point. Those tagged attempt to tag as many others as possible. The activity can continue until all but one have been poisoned.

This activity provides an opportunity for kinesthetic awareness as a child tries to keep from being pulled into the circle. Also, surface area resistance may be encountered, depending upon the type of surface where the activity takes place.

We Swing

This is a rhythmic activity and as such is concerned with body movement and the position of the body in space. It is the type of rhythmic activity that can make a child aware of the movement of certain muscle groups. The activity is in song-story form, and the parent and child together can make up a tune to it if they wish. Creative parents along with their children should be able to make up some of these kinds of activities on their own.

We hold hands (parents and child hold hands standing side by side.)
We will try to swing.
We swing our arms (parent and child swing both arms.)
We swing.
We swing.
We take four steps in (parent and child run four steps forward.)
We take four steps out (parent and child walk back four steps.)
We drop our hands.
We turn about.

Ball-Handling Activities

The ball-handling activities that were previously explained, when used with different sized balls, are of value as far as *timing* relates to kinesthetic perception. These activities are recommended for this purpose.

Tactile Perception

The tactile sense is very closely related to the kinesthetic sense, so much so in fact that these two senses are often confused. One of the main reasons for this is that the ability to detect changes in touch (tactile) involves many of the same receptors concerned with informing the body of changes in its position. The essential difference between the tactile sense and the kinesthetic sense may be seen in the definitions of kinesthetic and tactile perception. As stated previously, kinesthetic perception involves the mental interpretation of the sensation of movement, whereas tactile perception is concerned with the *mental interpretation of what a person experiences through the sense of touch.*

In addition to the importance of tactile stimulation as a essential factor in learning, another of its dimensions is that concerned with social interaction through tactile *communication.* Thus, the tactile sense not only has physical and psychological implications, but important sociological implications as well. It has been found that better human relations can be obtained with children through tactile communication in certain active play experiences that require touch, such as in the various tag games and holding hands in circle games. Some studies have shown that tactile communication in active play experiences provides a basis for attraction that is necessary for black and white children to form positive relationships. In fact, recorded incidents of tactile interaction between black children and white children are shown to be equilavent to the recorded incidents of tactile interaction between black children and black children and those between white children and white children.

Since the kinesthetic and tactile senses are so closely related, the identifying factors of deficiency in kinesthesis previously reported can also be used to determine if there is a deficiency in the tactile sense. Also, a number of elementary diagnostic techniques for tactile sensitivity can be played in a game type of situation so that the child is unaware of being tested. The following list suggests some representative examples, and creative parents are limited only by their own imagination in expanding the list:

1. Have the child explore the surface and texture of objects around the home. Determine if he can differentiate among these objects.
2. Evaluate the child's experience by having him give the names of two or three hard objects, two or three rough objects, and so on.
3. Make a *touching box* by using an ordinary shoe box. Place several differently shaped objects and differently textured objects in the box. Have the child reach into the box without looking, and have him feel the various objects to see if he can identify them.

Active Play Experiences Involving Tactile Perception

Children need tactile stimulation through touching and being touched. The following active play experiences, which involve touching and being touched, apply not only to tactile stimulation but also to tactile communication as a means of social interaction referred to previously.

Touch Something

In this activity the child runs around the activity area and touches differently textured objects called out by the parent. For example, the parent can say "Touch something hard," "Touch something rough," etc. The idea is to see how quickly the child can react and make the touch on the correct object. After a time the child should be given the opportunity to be the caller.

Electric Shock

This activity requires about five or more players who form a circle with one player designated as *It*. The player who is *It* stands inside the circle and attempts to determine where the *electric power* is concentrated. The players in the circle join hands, and one player is designated to start the electricity. This player accomplishes this by tightly squeezing the hand of the player on either side of him. As soon as a person's hand is squeezed, he keeps the electricity moving by squeezing the hand of the person next to him. If *It* thinks he knows where the electric power is, that is whose hand is being squeezed, he calls out that person's name. If *It* has guessed correctly, all of the players in the circle run to a previously designated safety area to avoid being tagged by him. If desired, a point can be scored against all those tagged, and the activity continues with another player becoming *It*. In this situation, the tactile sense becomes a medium of communication as each child's hand is squeezed by another.

Cat and Mouse

This activity requires several players, at least six or more. One child is chosen to be the mouse and another child is the cat. The remaining players join hands and form a circle, with the mouse in the center of the circle and the cat on the outside of the circle. The players in the circle try to keep the cat from getting into the circle and catching the mouse. If the cat gets inside the circle, the players in the circle let the mouse outside of the circle and try to keep the cat in, but they must keep their hands joined at all times. If the cat catches the mouse the activity is over, and those players join the circle while two others become the cat and mouse. If the mouse is not caught in a specified period of time, a new cat and mouse can be selected.

The players can see the importance of working together with joined hands. When the cat tries to enter the circle at a given point between two players, those two players can feel the tight grip of the hands needed to protect the mouse.

Stunt Play

Certain stunts provide fine possibilities for tactile perception in that some of them afford opportunities for body contact with others as well as with the surface area. Some representative examples of these kinds of activities follow.

Seal Crawl. In the Sea Crawl, the child supports himself on his hands while his body is extended back. The child squats and places his hands on the surface area shoulder width apart, palms flat, and fingers pointed forward. He extends his legs in back of himself until his body is straight. The child points his toes so that a part of his weight will be on the top of his feet. He is now ready to move forward on his hands, dragging his feet.

CHURN THE BUTTER. This activity involves two children about the same size. They turn back-to-back and lock elbows by bending their arms to approximately a 90 degree angle. The elbows are held in back of each performer, and the forearms are held against the ribs. One child picks up the other child from the surface area by bending forward with a slow, controlled movement. The other child will momentarily have his feet slightly off the surface area. The first child releases the lifting force by straightening to an erect standing position; the other child then lifts the first child in the same manner. This action is repeated as long as desired.

WHEELBARROW. A child has a partner of about equal size and strength. One of the pair assumes a position with his hands on the surface area, his elbows straight, and his feet extended behind him. The other chlid carries the feet of the first child, who keeps his knees straight. He becomes a wheelbarrow by walking on his hands. Positions are changed so that each can become the wheelbarrow.

Chapter Five

HOW TO HELP YOUR CHILD WITH
READING THROUGH ACTIVE PLAY

ONE of the very important school curriculum areas in the education of young children is the *language arts* program. This program includes listening, speaking, reading, and writing, all of which are concerned with communication. The primary purpose of the language arts in the modern elementary school is to facilitate communication.

Speaking and writing are sometimes referred to as the *expressive* phases of language, while listening and reading are considered the *receptive* phases. This implies that through speaking and writing the individual has the opportunity to express his or her own thoughts and feelings to others. Through reading and listening the individual receives the thoughts and feelings of others.

Although we have indicated that the language arts program contains listening, speaking, reading, and writing, the reader should not interpret this to mean that these are considered as entirely separate entities. On the contrary, they are closely interrelated, and each can be considered a component part of the broad area of communication. Such areas of study in the school as spelling, word meanings, and word recognition are involved in each of the four areas.

The importance of the interrelationship of the various language arts can be shown in different ways. For example, children must use words in speaking and have them meaningful before they can read them successfully. Also, they can spell better the words that they read with understanding and that they want to use for their own purposes. In addition, their handwriting even improves when they use it in purposeful and meaningful communication when someone they like is going to read it. Perhaps the two most closely interrelated and interdependent phases of the language arts are listening and reading. In fact, most reading specialists agree that learning to listen is the first step in learning to read. This relationship will be very apparent in many of our subsequent discussions in this chapter.

The modern elementary school gives a great deal of attention to this interrelationship of the various phases of the language arts. This is reflected in the way in which language experiences are being provided for children in the better-than-average elementary school. In the traditional elementary school it was a common practice to treat such aspects of the language arts as reading, writing, and spelling as separate subjects. As a result, they became more or less isolated and unrelated entities, and their full potential as media of expression probably was never fully realized. In the modern elementary school, where children have more freedom of expression and, consequently, greater opportunity for self-expression, the approach to teaching language arts is one that relates the various language areas to particular areas of interest. All of the phases of language arts — reading, listening, speaking, and writing — are thus used in the solution of problems in all curriculum areas. This procedure is primarily based upon the assumption that skill in communication should be developed in all of the activities engaged in by children.

We have already said that through reading the individual receives the thoughts and feelings of others; therefore, reading is considered a receptive phase of language. In this case the word *receptive* might well carry a figurative as well as purely literal meaning. Indeed, reading has been on the "receiving end" of a great deal of criticism during the past few years. Perhaps more criticism has been directed at it than all of the other school subjects combined. Although it may be difficult to determine precisely why reading has suffered the brunt of attack, one could speculate that it might be because, in general, most people consider reading as the real test of learning. In fact, in the early days of American education, grade levels tended to be thought of as "readers": a child was said to be in the "first reader," "second reader," and so on.

In modern times a good bit of the controversy involving reading seems to center around two general areas. First, there has been criticism of the various methods of teaching, reading, and second, there has been some question regarding the validity of the principles upon which these methods are based. Perhaps because of individual differences, any method used in absolute form to the exclusion of all other methods would not meet the needs of all children. For this reason it seems logical to assume that the procedures or combination of procedures employed should be those which best meet the needs of an individual child or a particular group of children.

It is *not* our purpose here to extol or criticize any of the past or present methods of teaching reading. Rather, the discussions in this chapter are intended to show how active play experiences can be used to assist the child in his or her efforts to read.

The theory that there is a high degree of relationship between participation in active play and reading is not new. For example, Fénelon, the famous French educator of the seventeenth century, is reputed to have said that he had seen certain children who had learned to read while playing. Although we do not know exactly what the gentleman meant, it could be speculated that his statement might well have been one of the first indications that there is a high level of compatibility between reading and active play, and a possible forerunner of some of the things we will expound in this chapter.

In any event, in modern times many tend to believe that the *kinesthetic* sense — the sense of "feel" they get through their muscles in active play — seems to be highly developed, and it helps children remember words they would take much longer to learn by looking at or sounding out. Moreover, practically all modern educators subscribe to the notion that children will learn more easily if the subject matter is something in which they are personally involved. Without question, active play experiences are extremely important to children and "are something that they are personally involved in." Consequently, reading that uses the medium of active play as a motivating factor can be very appealing to children. Subsequent discussions in the chapter will take many of these specific kinds of experiences into account. However, before getting directly into learning about reading through active play, it seems appropriate to discuss certain general aspects of the area of reading, and the following comments are intended for this purpose.

THE NATURE OF READING

Practically all of us learn to read, but of course with varying degrees of proficiency. Yet, to define exactly what reading means is not an easy task. A part of the reason for this is that it means different things to different people. It has been suggested that the psychologist thinks of reading as a thought process. Those who deal in semantics, which is the study of meanings, think of reading as the graphic representation of speech. The linguist, one who specializes in speech and language, is concerned with the sounds of language and its written form. Finally, the sociologist is concerned with the interaction of reading and culture.

We have already indicated that reading is an aspect of communication. As such, reading becomes more than just being able to recognize a word on a printed page. To communicate, a meaning must be shared and the reader must be able to comprehend. Thus, one of the most important concerns in teaching reading is that of helping children develop comprehension skills.

Reading could be thought of as bringing meaning *to* the printed page instead of only gaining meaning *from* it. This means that the author of a reading selection does not necessarily convey ideas to the reader but stimulates him to construct them out of his own experiences. (This is one of the major purposes of our program called the APAV Technique, which will be dealt with in detail later in the chapter.)

Since reading is such a complex act and it cannot be easily defined, we will resort to a rather broad and comprehensive description of the term. Our description of reading is an *interpretation of written or printed verbal symbols.* This can range from graffitti on restroom walls to the Harvard Classics.

It should be borne in mind that the entire child reads; he reads with his senses, his experiences, his cultural heritage, and of course with his muscles. It is the latter aspect with which we are predominantly concerned here because the aspect of "muscle sense" involved in active play is an extremely important dimension in reading for children.

WHEN TO BEGIN READING INSTRUCTION

Traditionally, the standard practice has been to begin the teaching of reading when children enter first grade at about six years of age. However, in recent years there appears to be a great deal of sentiment to start reading instruction before that time. A part of the reason for this is that there is a general feeling that young children are becoming more mature and possess more experience at an earlier age than was the case in the past. As a result of this prevailing belief, fully one-third of the teachers at the kindergarten level feel that their children can benefit from various forms of reading instruction. In fact, a large majority of kindergarten teachers conduct some of the fundamental phases of reading instruction, and only about 20 percent of them do not believe that reading instruction should be a part of the school program at that level.

A question that must be raised is "Does early reading instruction have any value?" Completely solid evidence to support one position or another is lacking to make an unqualified valid conclusion. One very important consideration is whether or not early instruction benefits the child as far as his total development is concerned. Some child development specialists feel that such instruction, if too highly structured and formalized, can actually cause harm to some children as far as their emotional development and social adjustment are concerned. One of the glorious features of using the active play approach as a form of parental tutoring in reading is the lack of formality and the application of creative and spontaneous experiences that are so important to the total developmental process.

READING READINESS

Closely allied to the problem of when to begin reading instruction is the question of reading readiness. There are certain *developmental tasks* that are important for children to accomplish. Reading can be considered as such a developmental task. That is, it is a task that a child needs to perform to satisfy his personal needs as well as those requirements which society and the culture impose upon him. In viewing reading as a developmental task, we can then consider reading readiness as a developmental *stage* at which certain factors have prepared the child for reading.

At one time, reading readiness was considered only as being concerned with the child being ready to *begin* the reading experience. In more recent years it has come to be thought of more in terms of each step of reading as one concerned with readiness for further reading. Therefore, the idea of reading readiness is not confined only to the start of reading instruction, but to the teaching and learning of most all reading skills. A given child may be considered ready to *learn to read* at a certain age. However, this same child may not necessarily be ready to *read to learn* until a later time. In fact, some reading specialists consider the primary level of grades one through three as a time for learning to read, and the intermediate level of grades four through six as a time when the child begins to read to learn.

Reading readiness needs to be thought of as a complex combination of basic abilities and conditions and not only as a single characteristic. This combination includes (1) various aspects of visual ability, (2) certain factors concerned with the auditory sense, (3) sex differences, (4) age, and (5) socioeconomic conditions. Obviously, it is not our purpose here to go into detail with reference to these various characteristics, but merely to identify them at this point. Later in the chapter, specific recommendations will be made concerning the application and function of active play as a medium for dealing with certain aspects of reading readiness.

DIAGNOSIS THROUGH ACTIVE PLAY

A standard general description of the term *diagnosis* is the act of identifying a condition from its signs and symptoms. Applied to reading, diagnosis implies an analysis of reading behavior for purposes of discovering strengths and weaknesses of a child as a basis for more effective guidance of his reading efforts.

Among other things, it is important for us to try to discover why a child reads as he does, what he is able to read, and what he reads successfully. In addition, we need to know if he is having problems in reading, what these problems are, and the causes of the problems.

In the school situation many diagnostic tests are available for use, and they have various degrees of validity. Studies tend to show that teachers themselves can forecast reading success of first grade children with about as much accuracy as reading readiness tests. It may be that such success in teacher observation has been a part of the reason for what is called *diagnostic teaching* becoming today's byword as school systems address their attention to meeting the needs of individual children. Diagnostic teaching simply means that teachers employ observation, recording, and analysis of children's performance in day-to-day reading situations.

Admittedly, the average parent will have little skill in the above techniques. Nevertheless, he or she can determine, at least to some extent, certain strengths and weaknesses that a child may manifest in active play situations. Thus, we will confine our discussion of a diagnosis through active play to attempts to assess a child's level of reading readiness.

Diagnosis of Reading Readiness Skills

Reading readiness skills are a complex cluster of basic skills including (1) language development in which the child learns to transform *his experience* with *his environment* into language symbols through listening, oral language facility and a meaningful vocabulary; (2) the skills relating to the mechanics of reading such as left-to-right orientation, auditory and visual discrimination, and recognition of letter names and sounds; and (3) the cognitive processes of comparing, classifying, ordering, interpreting, summarizing, and imagining.

Likewise, sensorimotor skills, meaning the functioning in both sensory and motor aspects of bodily activity, provide a foundation for these basic skills by sharpening the senses and developing motor skills involving spatial, form, and time concepts. The following outline identifies some concepts developed through direct body movement inherent in active play.

(The reader should note that most of these items were discussed in the previous chapter, where they were concerned with the improvement of general learning ability through active play. They are repeated here for purposes of continuity and also because they have direct application for reading readiness.)

1. Body Image
2. Space and Direction
3. Balance
4. Basic Body Movements
5. Eye-Hand Coordination
6. Eye-Foot Coordination
7. Form Perception
8. Rhythm
9. Large Muscle Activity
10. Fine Muscle Activity

These skills are important to the establishment of a sound foundation for the beginning-to-read experiences of children. Not only can reading readiness experiences, structured for the development of these skills, be facilitated through active play situations, but diagnosis of progress in skill development can be obtained by parent-tutor observation and a child's self-evaluation from the active play experiences. The following active play situations are described to indicate a variety of active play experiences that may be employed by the parent in the development and assessment of readiness skills.

Language Development

In the following active play experiences, concept formation is translated into meaningful vocabulary.

Concept: Vocabulary Meaning — Word Opposites
Activity: I'm Tall, I'm Small

In a one-to-one situation, the parent and child stand facing each other a short distance apart. They both walk around the room singing or saying the following verse:

I'm tall, I'm very small
I'm small, I'm very tall,

Sometimes I'm tall,
Sometimes I'm small
Tell what I am now.

As the child and parent walk around and sing "tall," "very tall," or "small," "very small" they stretch up or stoop down, depending on the words. At the end of the singing, they assume the position they were in at the time. If the parent wishes to participate with other members of the family or with other playmates as a group, a circle can be formed and one child stands in the center of the circle with eyes closed. The same procedure is followed, but at the end, the child in the center tries to guess the position of the others before opening his eyes.

This activity helps a child develop word meaning by acting out the words. Use of word opposites in this manner helps to dramatize the differences in the meaning of words. The words and actions can be changed to incorporate a large number of "opposites":

My hands are near, my hands are far.
Now they're far, now they're near.
Sometimes they're near.
Sometimes they're far.
Tell what they are now.

Concept: Vocabulary Meaning — Action Words
Activity: What to Play
The parent and child stand a few feet apart; the parent can act as the leader and can recite or sing the following verse to the tune of "Mary Had a Little Lamb."

(Name of child) tell us what to play,
What to play, what to play,
(Name) tell us what to play,
Tell us what to play.

The parent can then say "Let's play we're fishes," or "Let's wash dishes," or any other thing that depicts action. The parent performs the action and the child imitates. This can also be played with several persons as well as just the parent and child.

This activity gives children an opportunity to act out meanings of words. It helps them to recognize that spoken words represent actions of people as well as things that can be touched.

Concept: Vocabulary Meaning — Left and Right
Activity: Changing Seats

The parent and child each have several chairs that are placed side by side. The parent calls "Change right!" and the child moves into the seat at this right. The parent can bring excitement into the activity by the quickness of commands or unexpectedness by calling the same direction several times in succession. This activity can easily be performed with a group as well as with only two individuals.

This type of activity makes children more aware of the necessity of differentiating left from right. In the early stages, children may not be able to differentiate directions rapidly, or maybe not at all. The parent will need to gear the rapidity of the commands to the skill of the child. In some cases the parent can also move so that the child can see the direction of the move.

Concept: Classification
Activity: Pet Store

This activity requires several players such as other family members or playmates. One fairly large Pet Store is marked off at one end of the activity area and a Home at the other end. At the side is an area designated as a Cage. In the center of the playing area stands the Pet Store Owner. All of the players in the Pet Store are given a picture of one kind of pet (for example, fish, dog, cat, bird). These can be cut out of magazines or drawn by the parents and children. There should be about two or three pictures of each kind of pet. The Pet Store Owner calls "Fish" (or any of the other pets in the game). The children who have the pictures of fish must try to run from the Pet Store to their new Home without being caught or tagged by the Owner. If they are caught, they must go to the Cage and wait for the next call. The game continues until all the Pets have tried to get to their new Home. Kinds of pets can be changed frequently.

By grouping themselves according to the animal pictures,

children are able to practice classifying things that swim, things that fly, and so forth.

Auditory Discrimination

Concept: Auditory Discrimination — Beginning Sounds of
     Words
Activity: Man from Mars

This activity requires several players, although as few as three could play it. One child is selected to be the Man from Mars and stands in the center of the activity area. The others stand behind a designated line at one end of the play area. The game begins when the children call out "Man from Mars, can we chase him through the stars?" The parent answers, "Yes, if your names begins like duck" (or any other word). All the children whose names begin with the same beginning sound as *duck*, or whatever word is called, chase the Man from Mars until he is caught. The child who tags him becomes the new Man from Mars, and the game can continue.

For the children to run at the right time, they must listen carefully and match beginning sounds. If the parent sees a child not running when he should, individual help can be given.

Concept: Auditory Discrimination — Auditory-Motor Associa-
     tion
Activity: I Say Stoop

The parent acting as the leader stands facing the child a short distance away. The parent says either "I say stoop" or "I say stand." The parent carries out the action, but the child must carry out the command rather than the action. For example, if the parent says "I say stand" and stoops, the child, if he fails to follow the command but follows the action, could have a point scored against him if a score is kept. The position is reversed and the child is given a turn at being the leader. This game is adaptable to a group by having a leader and several players.

Many opposite action or direction words could be used, such as in and out, stop and go, run and walk, up and down, forward and backward, and so on. This activity not only provides for alertness in auditory-motor association but also can give practice in recognition of word opposites.

Visual Discrimination

Concept: Visual Discrimination
Activity: Giant Step

The child (or children if a group is involved) stands at the back of a small area with a finish line a given distance away. The parent uses pictures cut from magazines; if desired, these can be pasted on cards. The cards are of object pairs, similar and different. One pair of cards is held up. If the paired objects or symbols are the same, the child takes a giant step forward. It should be observed to see the child's reaction if he is shown an unpaired set of cards. When the game is played with several individuals it can be seen who gets to the finish line first.

Concept: Visual Discrimination — Visual-Motor Coordination
Activity: Jump the Shot

The parent holds a length of rope with an object tied to one end. The object should be something soft such as a yarn ball or bean bag. The parent starts by swinging the rope around in a circle close to the feet of the child and slightly above the surface area. The child attempts to avoid being hit by the object by jumping over it when it goes by. With several players a circle can be formed with the parent in the center of the circle, and the same procedure is used.

This activity provides a good opportunity for visual-motor coordination as a child must quickly coordinate his movement with the visual experience. The parent should observe to see how well the child makes the judgments necessary to jump over the object at the proper time.

Concept: Visual Discrimination
Activity: Match Cards

This activity is best when there are several players. Each player in the group is given a different-colored card. Several players are given duplicate cards. There are two chairs placed in the center of the activity area. On a signal the players may walk, skip, etc. to musical accompaniment. When the music stops the parent holds up a card. Those players whose cards match the parent's card run to sit in the chairs. Anyone who gets a seat can be given a point. Play resumes and the cards should be exchanged frequently among the players.

HELPING YOUR CHILD WITH READING SKILLS THROUGH ACTIVE PLAY

For the most part, the development of successful reading ability is dependent upon the extent to which a child acquires various basic *reading skills*. There does not appear to be complete agreement among reading specialists on the terminology used to identify these basic reading skills. Neither do they agree entirely on how such skills should be classified. It has been our pleasure to collaborate on various projects with some of the most outstanding reading specialists in the United States. It is from these sources that we derive our descriptions of terminology and classifications. In this regard, it will be the intent of this section of the chapter to present active play situations that can be used effectively by parents to develop skills in the areas of *sight vocabulary, word analysis skills,* and *comprehension*.

Sight Vocabulary

Sight vocabulary is concerned with being able to recognize a word on sight. Ordinarily, children may be expected to be able to identify a certain number of words on sight before they are introduced to the more complicated process of word analysis. However, there is a wide variation in recommendations of the number of sight words a child should acquire. This ranges from learning three or four words by sight to 100 or more words. Of course, this would be concerned with the age and ability level of each individual child.

The parent should be aware that the learning of sight words involves *sounding*; thus, the importance of *saying* a word is emphasized. Some reading specialists go so far as to consider it as a *seeing, saying,* and *comprehending* process. The following active play experiences take these recommendations into account.

Concept: Sight Vocabulary

Activity: Find the Place

The parent prepares a number of cards with a lettered word on each card. Let us say that on one of the cards is the word *chair*. The parent holds up the card and calls out "Chair!" The child runs to a chair. If the child does not associate the object, assistance can be given. The parent might wish to give a clue such as "something to sit on." Many different kinds of words can be used.

Concept: Sight Vocabulary
Activity: Jump on the word

The parent takes a large piece of cloth such as an old bed sheet. Lines are drawn on the sheet to make six to nine sections. In each section a word is lettered. The child stands at the edge of the sheet. The parent holds up a picture of one of the words printed on the sheet. At the same time, the parent calls out the word and the child jumps on it. For example, if the word is "tree," a picture of a tree is held up and the word is called out. As in the case of the previous activity, assistance can be given as needed. This activity also helps children associate picture clues with words.

Concept: Sight Vocabulary
Activity: Look for the Word

The same word cards for "Find the Place" can be used for this activity; however, a duplicate set is also needed. The parent places the cards on the surface area with the child a short distance away. The parent holds up a card and calls out the name of the word. The child runs to the pile of cards to look for the word.

Concept: Sight Vocabulary
Activity: Word Carpet

The parent prepares a list of words on a long piece of cardboard or portable chalkboard if one is available. Several individual pieces of cardboard with these words written on them are placed on the surface area to represent Word Carpets. The parent gives a signal to "go" and the child skips all around the surface on the Word Carpets. When the parent gives a signal to "stop," the parent calls out the word and the child identifies the word he is standing on or closest to from the list on the board.

Note: In the above activities the parent should involve the child in saying the word and must decide in which way this will be most profitable. Parents can derive words from children's stories and readers. In addition, standard vocabulary word lists for the different age levels can probably be obtained from the local school.

Word Analysis

The terms *word analysis, word recognition* and *word attack* appear to be used interchangably to mean essentially the same thing when applied to the skills of reading. It should be understood that we cannot rely indefinitely upon sight vocabulary as a means of learning and remembering the literally thousands of words needed for reading. Therefore, efforts are made in the schools to begin rather early to develop skills that help the child to learn vocabulary. Thus, it is the general function of word analysis skills to allow the child to progress faster in vocabulary development than would be the case if he had to learn each new word by sight.

Among other things, word analysis is concerned with such factors as letter recognition, auditory and visual discrimination, auditory-visual association, vowel letter patterns, syllabication, affixes, accent, and alphabetical order. Following are many suitable active play experiences that parents can use to help in the development of word analysis skills.

Concept: Recognizing Letters of the Alphabet
Activity: Letter Snatch

The child stands about 10 to 12 feet away from an object such as a ball or beanbag. The child is given a card with a letter on it. The parent has several cards with different letters. One of the cards is held up, and if it is the same letter the child has, he runs and sees how fast he can get the object. The child's cards are changed frequently. The parent should be alert to see on which letters most practice is needed. With several players they can be divided into two groups with members of each group given like letters. When a letter is held up, the two players having that letter try to run and retrieve the object.

Concept: Each sound has a definite form, and each form has a
      definite sound (auditory-visual perception)
Activity: Stop, Look, and Listen

The child stands a given distance away and facing the parent.
The parent holds up a card with a letter of the alphabet. At the
same time, the parent calls out a word that *does* or *does not*
begin with that sound. If the word does begin with the sound,
the child runs to where the parent is standing. If the word does
not begin with the sound the child does not run.

Concept: Recognizing Letters of the Alphabet — Vowels
Activity: Magic Vowels

This activity is much like Word Carpet except that the
"carpets" have vowels on them instead of words, and these are
called Magic Vowels. At a signal to "go," the child skips
around on the Magic Vowels. At the signal to stop from the
parent the child tries to name the vowel he is standing on. If
able to do so he can be awarded a point with a certain number
of points needed to complete the game. This activity can provide practice in the recognition of vowel letters.

Concept: Auditory Discrimination — Beginning Sounds in
      Words
Activity: Match the Sound

The child skips around the surface area until the parent gives
a signal to stop. The parent then says a word, at the same time
tossing a ball to the child. The parent begins to count to ten.
Before the parent finishes counting, the child must say another
word that begins with the same sound. Again, points can be
scored if so desired. This activity enables the child to listen for
sounds in the initial position of words. It can also be adapted
to listening for final position sounds.

Concept: Auditory Discrimination — Consonant Blends
Activity: Crows and Cranes

This activity requires several players. The playing area is
divided by a center line. The players are divided into two teams.
There should probably be a minimum of three or four on each
team. The players on one team are designated as Crows and
take a position on one side of the playing area. The members of

the other team are designated as Cranes and take a position on the other side of the playing area. The far baseline of each team is the safety zone. At the start the Crows and Cranes are about 3 feet apart. The parent calls our "Cr-r-anes" or "Cr-r-ows." The initial consonant blend "Cr" is emphasized. If the parent calls "Crows," they turn and run to their baseline to avoid being tagged. The Cranes attempt to tag their opponents before they cross their baseline. The Cranes score a point for each Crow tagged. They return to their places and the parent proceeds to call one of the groups, and play continues in the same manner. The game can be extended to include other words beginning with consonant blends, for example, swans and swallows, storks and starlings, squids and squabs.

Repetition of the consonant blends during the game helps children to become aware of these sounds and to develop their auditory perception of the blends in the context of words. Discovering names of animals with other consonant blends can help children in their ability to hear consonant blends in the initial position of words.

Concept: Auditory Discrimination — Consonant Blends
Activity: Call Blends

The parent stands a given distance away from the child and holds a ball. The child is given an initial consonant blend by the parent (*st, gr, bl, cl,* and so forth). The parent calls out a word with an initial consonant blend and tosses the ball into the air. If it is the blend the child has been given, he tries to run and retrieve the ball on the first bounce. Each time the child is given a different consonant blend. The parent should be alert to see those consonant blends with which the child needs help.

Concept: Auditory Discrimination — Final Consonant Blends
(*nk, ck, nd, st, nt, rst*)
Activity: Final Blend Change

This activity requires several players. The players form a single circle, with one player standing in the center of the circle. The players in the circle are designated as different final consonant blends. Each player may be given a card with his blend written on it to help him remember. The parent then pronounces a word with one of the final position blends. All of the players with this blend must hold up their card and then run to exchange places. The player in the center tries to get one of the vacant places in the circle. The remaining player goes to the center. In this game, children must listen carefully to the word pronounced. By holding up their card, they are associating the visual with the auditory symbol for that sound.

Concept: Auditory Discrimination — Vowels
Activity: Vowels in a Basket

For this activity a wastebasket and an object such as a beanbag or yarn ball are needed. The object of the game is for the child to give a word with a different vowel from the one in the word the parent calls, for example, *bed-bad, hip-hop, had-hid,* and to toss the object into the wastebasket. A point can be scored for a correct medial vowel substitution and another point for a successful throw.

Children need practice in working with medial vowels in the context of meaningful words. The parent can reinforce the vowels used in the words by writing down each set of words so the child can see the vowels in context. To make the game more difficult, the parent can also ask the child to identify which vowel was in the word that was called and in the word given by the child. For children having difficulty in hearing vowel sounds, another adaptation might be to use familiar sight vocabulary words and print them on large-size cards. The parent can display the word and say the word at the same time.

Concept: Rhyming Words
Activity: Rhyme Grab

An object such as a ball or beanbag is placed on the playing area a given distance away from the child. The parent then gives the child a word. The parent then calls out a word. If this word rhymes with the child's word, the child runs out and grabs the object. If desired, some sort of point scheme can be devised with so many points needed to complete a game.

Children need to have many opportunities that call upon their auditory skill in hearing words that rhyme. In this game, the child may also be given an opportunity to associate printed words with the spoken words by having the parent alternate holding up word cards and the child determining if the word rhymes with the printed word, or giving the child a word card and having the parent call out words.

Concept: Alphabetical Order
Activity: Alphabet Throw

The parent cuts five pieces of cardboard, in the shape of circles, about 12 inches in diameter. A letter of the alphabet is marked in each circle. The letters in the circles need not necessarily be placed in correct order, but they should be a series of letters (*A, B, C, D, E* or *H, I, J, K, L*). The child is given five beanbags or yarn balls. The child throws the first beanbag toward the circle with the first letter according to its alphabetical order, then the second, and so on. One point can be given for each bag that lands within the circle in correct alphabetical order (bag 1 in *A*, bag 2 in *B*, bag 3 in *C*, and so on).

In this game, the child is provided the practice in using the skills in putting letters in alphabetical order. By changing the letter after each game, the child becomes familiar with various parts of the alphabet. When changing letters, the parent might add and delete only a couple of letters rather than using a complete new set of letters.

Comprehension

As important as sight vocabulary and word analysis skills are in reading, the bottom line, so to speak, is comprehension. Without it, reading is reduced simply to the "calling of words." Many people have difficulty defining comprehension as it applies to reading. We like to think of it as the process of correctly associating meaning with word symbols, or simply extracting meaning from the written or printed page. Comprehension also involves evaluation of this meaning, sorting out the correct meaning, and organizing ideas as a selection is read. In addition, there should be retention of these ideas for possible use or reference in some future endeavor.

To accomplish comprehension as described here, it is important for children to develop certain comprehension skills. The following is a list of such *general* comprehension skills.

1. Getting Facts
2. Selecting Main Ideas

3. Organizing Main Ideas by Enumeration and Sequence
4. Following Directions
5. Drawing Inferences
6. Gaining Independence in Word Mastery
7. Building a Meaningful Vocabulary
8. Distinguishing Fact from Fantasy

In the final section of the chapter, "Active Play Reading Content," we will show how this list of comprehension skills can be used as an inventory for the parent to evaluate how well the child is practicing and maintaining comprehension skills in listening and/or reading.

The following active play experiences are some representative ways in which the parent can assist the child in developing comprehension. Some of the activities are concerned with general comprehension, while others are more specific in nature.

Concept: Vocabulary Meaning — On, Up, Down, Over, Under, Front, Back
Activity: Do What It Says

The parent prepares word cards using the above words. The child responds to the sight of the word on the card and the calling of the word by the parent. The parent may say "Go *under* the table," at the same time displaying the word card. The parent can use the words in various ways depending upon the kind of objects and situations available in an inside or outside area where the activity takes place.

Concept: Following Directions
Activity: Simon Says

The parent stands a given distance away, facing the child. To begin with, the parent takes the part of Simon. Later these positions can be reversed so that the child gets a turn at being Simon. Every time Simon says something, the child must do it. However, if a command is given without the prefix "Simon Says," the child must remain motionless. For example, when "Simon says take two steps," the child must take two steps. But, if Simon says "Walk backward two steps," the child should not move. If desirable, some sort of scoring system can be devised to record the number of correct and incorrect responses.

This activity provides the child the opportunity to follow oral directions in a highly motivating situation. This is also a good activity for use with several players.

Concept: Following Directions
Activity: Do This, Do That

Cards with the words "Do This" and "Do That" are used in this activity. The parent stands in front of the child a given distance away. The parent holds up a card and makes a movement such as running in place or swinging the arms. The child follows the action of the parent when the card says "Do This." When the parent holds up the card sign that says "Do That," the child must not move although the parents continues the action. Again, a point system can be devised if so desired, and the parent and child can take turns at being the leader.

This activity can be used to help the child to read carefully so as to follow directions. This game can be made more advanced later by having the parent display written directions such as hop in place, jump once, run in place, etc. This is also a good activity for use with several players.

Concept: Classification
Activity: Ducks Fly

The parent stands in front of the child a given distance away. The parent names different things that can fly such as ducks, birds, and airplanes. As the parent calls out, "Ducks fly, Birds fly, Airplanes fly," he or she moves the arms as if flying. The child follows as long as the parent names something that can fly. If the parent says "Elephants fly," and although the parent continues to keep the arms moving as in flying, the child must stop moving his own arms. If desired, some sort of point system can be devised for scoring. As in the case of similar activities, the parent and child can alternate being the leader.

Children need to develop the skill of classifying things into groups having common characteristics. A child should be helped to notice that some animals actually can do several of the movements named as flying, walking, and/or swimming. This activity can be followed up by having the child collect pictures of animals and make a display of animals who walk, swim, etc.

Concept: Vocabulary Meaning
Activity: Word Hunt

The parent prepares a box of pictures, which can be cut from magazines. Also prepared is a set of word cards corresponding to the pictures. The word sets are placed in a flat box near a place on the playing area that can be called a "sentence chart." The child selects a picture from the box. On a signal he runs to the word-set box and looks for the word to match the picture. Then he places the word and picture on the sentence chart. He then returns to his original starting point and repeats the performance with another picture. This can continue until all the pictures and words have been matched.

Emphasis on word meaning is provided in this activity. The child is helped to visualize the concept that a word represents through pictures.

Concept: Vocabulary Meaning — Action Words
Activity: Word Action

The parent prepares a number of action words on cards and places them in a box. The child takes a word from the box, shows it to the parents, and then tries to act out the word. If the child does not know the word, the parent should tell him. If desired, a point can be scored for every word acted out correctly.

This activity helps the child gain the meaning of words by providing him with means of visualizing and feeling the action represented by the word. The child can also gain the concept that words represent not only specific objects they can see and touch but also actions that can be observed.

ACTIVE PLAY READING CONTENT

The term *reading content* is easy to describe because it is simply concerned with the information that a given reading selection contains. Therefore, active play reading content provides for reading material that is oriented to active play situations. Stories of different lengths are prepared for various readability levels, and the content focuses upon any aspect of active play. Content can be concerned with such forms of active play as games, stunts, rhythmic activities, and creative experiences.

One of the early, and possibly the first, attempts to prepare active play reading content — at least as conceived here — is the work of the first author of this book. This work, begun in the early 1960s, involved preparation of a number of active play stories. These stories were used with several hundred children, and on the basis of the findings of the studies, the following generalizations have been derived:

1. When a child is self-motivated and interested, he reads. In this case, the reading was done without the usual motivating devices such as pictures, clues, and illustrations.
2. These active play stories were found to be extremely successful in stimulating interest in reading and at the same time improving the child's ability to read.
3. Because the material for these active play stories was scientifically selected, prepared, and tested, it is unique in the field of children's independent reading material. The outcomes have been most satisfactory in terms of children's interest in reading content of this nature as well as motivation to read.

From Listening to Reading

Before we get directly into the use of active play reading content, we need to take into account the important relationship between listening and reading. An important thing to remember is that the comprehension skills for listening are the same as the comprehension skills for reading. (see list of comprehension skills on pages 97-98). The essential difference in these two receptive phases of language is in the form of *input* that is used. That is, listening is dependent upon the *auditory* (hearing) sense, and reading is dependent upon the *visual* (seeing) sense. Since the main goal of reading is comprehension, it is important to recognize that as children listen to active play situations and react to them, they are developing essential skills for reading.

This brings us to the important question, "Should parents read to their children?" People who spend their time studying about this reply with an unqualified affirmative. That is, there seems to be solid evidence to support the idea that reading to children improves their vocabulary knowledge, reading comprehension, interest in reading, and the general quality of language development. We emphasize this at this point, because we shall see later that reading to children is an important dimension in the use of active play reading content.

THE APAV TECHNIQUE

Our procedure for learning to read through the use of active play reading content is identified as the *APAV Technique,* several examples of which will be presented later. The APAV Technique involves a learning sequence of *auditory input* to *play* to *auditory-visual input,* as depicted in the following diagram.

*A*uditory   *P*lay   *A*uditory-*V*isual

Essentially, this technique is a procedure for working through active play to develop comprehension first in listening and then in reading. The A$\longrightarrow$P aspect of APAV is a directed listening-thinking activity. The child first receives the thoughts and feelings expressed in an active play story through the auditory sense by listening to the story read by the parent. Following this, the child engages in the active play experiences that are inherent in the story, and thereby demonstrates understanding of and reaction to the story. By engaging in the active play experience, the development of comprehension becomes a part of the child's physical reality.

After the active play experience in the directed listening-thinking activity, the child moves to the final aspect of the APAV Technique (A-V), a combination of auditory and visual experience by listening to the story read by the parent and *reading along* with the parent. In this manner, comprehension is brought to the reading experience.

Although the sequence of listening to reading is a natural one, bridging the gap to the point of handling the verbal symbols required in reading poses various problems for many children. One of the outstanding features of the APAV Technique is that the active play experience helps to serve as a bridge between listening and reading by providing direct purposeful experience for the child through active play after listening to the story.

Following are several examples of stories that the parent can use in applying the APAV Technique. Remember, first you read the story to the child, then with various degrees of parental guidance he participates in the active play experience, and then you and the child read the story together. This technique may be used with your school age children who are encountering some difficulties with comprehension, and it can be used with your immediate preschool child to help him gain some sight words and develop listening skills. As far as the latter is concerned, we have had very successful experience with four to five year old children, finding that many of them can retain what they have listened to for a minimum of one week and sometimes even much longer.

THE FUNNY CLOWN

I AM A FUNNY CLOWN.

I MOVE LIKE A FUNNY CLOWN.

I JUMP.

I SKIP.

I RUN.

I STOP.

I HAVE FUN.

CIRCUS ELEPHANT

I SAW THE CIRCUS.

I SAW MANY ANIMALS.

I SAW AN ELEPHANT.

HE WAS BIG.

HE HAD BIG LEGS.

HE TOOK BIG STEPS.

HE HAD A TRUNK.

HE SWINGS HIS TRUNK.

I WILL WALK LIKE THE ELEPHANT.

CURLY CAT TAKES A WALK

CURLY CAT IS ASLEEP.

CURLY OPENS HIS EYES.

CURLY CAT TAKES A WALK.

HE WALKS WITH LONG STEPS.

HE HOLDS HIS HEAD HIGH.

HE WALKS ALL AROUND.

TRY TO WALK LIKE CURLY CAT.

PUT YOUR HANDS ON THE FLOOR.

WALK ALL AROUND LIKE CURLY CAT.

GRIZZLY BEAR

I SAW A GRIZZLY BEAR.

GRIZZLY BEAR WAS AT THE ZOO.

HE WALKED AND WALKED.

HE WALKED AROUND HIS CAGE.

I CAN WALK LIKE GRIZZLY BEAR.

I CAN PUT MY HANDS ON THE FLOOR.

I WALK ON MY HANDS AND FEET.

I WALK AND WALK.

I SAY, "GR-GR-GR."

THE JUMPING RABBIT

I CAN JUMP LIKE A RABBIT.

I SIT LIKE A RABBIT.

I HOLD MY HANDS ON THE FLOOR.

NOW I JUMP.

MY FEET COME UP TO MY HANDS.

I HOLD MY HANDS WAY OUT.

I PUT MY HANDS ON THE FLOOR.

I JUMP AGAIN.

I JUMP AGAIN AND AGAIN.

THE SPIDER

HAVE YOU EVER WATCHED THE WAY SPIDERS WALK?

THEY HAVE LONG LEGS.

THEY PUT THEM WAY OUT.

TRY TO WALK LIKE A SPIDER.

PUT YOUR HANDS ON THE FLOOR.

KEEP YOUR ARMS STRAIGHT.

WALK TO THE FRONT.

WALK TO ONE SIDE.

WALK TO THE OTHER SIDE.

WALK TO THE BACK.

WALK ALL AROUND LIKE A SPIDER.

THE LAME PUPPY

I SAW A LAME PUPPY.

THE LAME PUPPY WALKED.

HE HELD UP ONE LEG.

HE WALKED ON THREE LEGS.

I WALK LIKE THIS PUPPY.

I HOLD UP ONE LEG.

I WALK ON ONE LEG AND TWO HANDS.

I WALK AROUND.

CASPER CAMEL

CASPER CAMEL LIVES IN THE ZOO.

HE HAS A HUMP ON HIS BACK.

COULD YOU LOOK LIKE CASPER CAMEL?

YOU WILL NEED A HUMP.

TRY IT THIS WAY.

BEND FORWARD.

PUT YOUR HANDS BEHIND YOUR BACK.

HOLD THEM TOGETHER.

THAT WILL BE A HUMP.

THAT WILL LOOK LIKE CASPER CAMEL.

COULD YOU MOVE LIKE CASPER CAMEL?

TAKE A STEP.

LIFT YOUR HEAD.

TAKE A STEP.

LIFT YOUR HEAD.

MOVE LIKE CASPER CAMEL.

FALLING LEAVES

LEAVES FALL.

THEY FALL FROM THE TREES.

THEY FALL TO THE GROUND.

FALL LIKE LEAVES.

DOWN, DOWN, DOWN.

DOWN TO THE GROUND.

QUIET LEAVES.

REST LIKE LEAVES.

THE GROWING FLOWERS

FLOWERS GROW.

FIRST THEY ARE SEEDS.

BE A SEED.

GROW LIKE A FLOWER.

GROW AND GROW.

KEEP GROWING.

GROW TALL.

NOW YOU ARE A FLOWER.

ROCKING CHAIR (FOR TWO CHILDREN)

THERE ARE MANY KINDS OF CHAIRS.

ONE KIND OF CHAIR IS A ROCKING CHAIR.

IT ROCKS AND ROCKS.

TWO CHILDREN CAN BECOME A ROCKING CHAIR.

THEY SIT FACING EACH OTHER.

THEY SIT ON EACH OTHER'S FEET.

THEY ROCK AND ROCK.

SAMMY SQUIRREL (FOR SEVERAL CHILDREN)

ONE DAY SAMMY SQUIRREL MET SOME FRIENDS.

THEY WANTED TO RUN AND PLAY.

SAMMY'S FRIENDS WENT TO ONE END OF THE FIELD.

SAMMY STAYED IN THE CENTER OF THE FIELD.

HE WAS *IT*.

WHEN SAMMY SAID "CHANGE," HIS FRIENDS RAN TO THE OTHER END.

SAMMY TRIED TO TAG THEM.

HE TAGGED ONE.

NOW HE WAS SAMMY'S HELPER.

SAMMY SAID "CHANGE," AGAIN.

THE SQUIRRELS RAN BACK TO THE OTHER END.

MORE SQUIRRELS WERE TAGGED.

THEY WERE SAMMY'S HELPERS.

EACH TIME SAMMY SAID "CHANGE," THEY RAN TO THE OTHER END.

THEY PLAYED UNTIL ONLY ONE SQUIRREL WAS LEFT.

HE WAS *IT* FOR THE NEXT GAME.

COULD YOU PLAY THIS GAME WITH YOUR FRIENDS?

Previously, we provided a list of general comprehension skills and indicated that we would show how this list could be used as an inventory to help the parent determine how well the child is practicing and maintaining comprehension skills for listening and/or reading.

Inventory of Listening and/or Reading Comprehension Skills
Directions: Check YES or NO to indicate proficiency or lack of proficiency with which the child is using skills.

SKILLS

Yes No

—— —— 1. Getting Facts — Does the child understand what to do and how to do it?

—— —— 2. Selecting Main Ideas — Does the child use succinct instructions in preparing for and doing the play activity?

—— —— 3. Organizing Main Ideas by Enumeration and Sequence — Does the child know the order in which the activity is performed?

—— —— 4. Following Directions — Does the child proceed with the activity according to the precise instructions in the story?

—— —— 5. Drawing Inferences — Does the child seem to draw reasonable conclusions as shown by the way he imitates the animal, person, or object in the story?

—— —— 6. Gaining Independence in Word Mastery — Does the child use word analysis to get a word without asking for help? (This applies only if child has been introduced to word analysis skills.)

—— —— 7. Building a Meaningful Vocabulary — Does the child use any of the words in the story in his speaking vocabulary as he proceeds in the active play experience?

—— —— 8. Distinguishing Fact from Fantasy — Does the child indicate which stories are real and which are imaginary, particularly as far as some of the characters are concerned?

It should be recognized that different children will develop comprehension skills at different rates. Therefore, the parent should be patient and provide cheerful parental guidance as needed in assisting the child in performing the active play experiences depicted in the stories.

It is entirely possible that some parents will want to try to develop some of their own active play reading content, and we heartily recommend that you try your hand at it. Should this be the case, the following guidelines are submitted for consideration.

1. In general, the *new* word load should be kept relatively low. (We mentioned previously that appropriate word lists can probably be obtained from the local school.)
2. When new words are used, there should be as much repetition of these words as possible and appropriate.
3. Sentence length and lack of complex sentences should be considered in keeping the level of difficulty of material within the ability levels of children.
4. Consideration must also be given to the reading values and literary merits of a story. Using a character or characters in a story setting helps to develop interest.
5. The activity to be used in the story should *not* be readily identifiable. When children identify an activity early in the story, there can be resulting minimum attention on their part to get the necessary details to engage in the active play experience. Thus, in developing an active play story, it is important that the nature of the activity and procedures for it unfold gradually.

In closing this chapter, we should say that we have attempted to show many possibilities available to parents through which they can help their child with reading through the medium of active play. We hope that these examples will be of use to you and also that you will be inspired to develop many additional experiences on your own.

Chapter Six

HOW TO HELP YOUR CHILD WITH MATHEMATICS THROUGH ACTIVE PLAY

THE subject of mathematics in today's elementary schools, with the never-ending attempts at new methods and changes in content, is bewildering not only to parents but to many conscientious teachers as well.

Over the years there have been many periods of change in mathematics in schools, and believe it or not, there was a time when mathematics was not even considered a proper subject of study for children. Since there is so much confusion about the subject of mathematics among parents and others, we feel that it is appropriate at the outset of this chapter to give a brief overview of "where we have been" and "where we think we are today" in mathematics.

In the very early days of this country the ability to compute was regarded as appropriate for a person doing menial work, but such skill was not viewed as appropriate for the aristocracy. Accordingly, the study of mathematics was not emphasized in the early schools of America, not even the study of arithmetic.* Gradually, as commerce increased, the ability to compute became increasingly valued, and arithmetic became a part of the general education of the young. In fact, it gained an equal place in the curriculum with religion, reading, and writing. In 1789, laws to make arithmetic a required school subject were passed in Massachusetts and New Hampshire. During this time in our history, arithmetic was used mainly by businessmen and very gradually came into the schools of the day. By 1800, arithmetic was taught quite generally in the schools.

---

*In the early 1960s the subject of arithmetic became more generally known as "elementary school mathematics." No doubt the reason for this was that at about this time elementary schools were beginning to include more advanced forms of the mathematical processes in addition to the traditional study of arithmetic. Arithmetic is concerned with numbers and the computation with them and is considered to be a branch of the broader area of mathematics.

Arithmetic, as taught during the early years of the new nation, consisted of "working problems from rules." Only the teacher had a book, and the rules presented were applied largely to problems of commerce of that day. Arithmetic was seldom taught to children below ten years of age. In fact, when a boy started to study the subject, it was considered a sign of approaching manhood.

For a good portion of the nineteenth century, much of arithmetic that was taught at the grade school level was characterized by large numbers of drill exercises. This was also accompanied by the false notion that the study of arithmetic was useful in "training the mind." It is not surprising that mathematics was viewed by large numbers of children as something to be dreaded, for exercises were deliberately designed to be difficult so as to better "exercise" the mind. For example, such problems as the following were commonly included in the arithmetic books of that day:

What is the cost of 7 1/8 tons of coal if .675 of a ton costs $5.235?

A man bought 5/6 of a box of apples, and after he and his family ate 3/4 of them, he sold the remainder for 8/9 of a dollar; how much would a full box cost at the same rate?

It was thought that such problems would help children think clearly and quickly. It is questionable whether today's instruction in mathematics has completely recovered from the accompanying dread of arithmetic and the idea that "difficult is good" and "fun must be bad."

As schools became graded during the late nineteenth century, textbooks also became graded. Whereas a single text had been sufficient, texts were written for each grade level. These graded texts resulted in more specific expectations at each level, locking teachers and children into material they were expected to cover. However, there were many who were seeking changes by the latter part of the century. The value of previous procedures was being questioned. Rather, attention was turning toward more practical values. The Child Study Movement was beginning to have an impact, and it is not surprising that the period from 1890 to 1911 has been thought of as a period of reflection in mathematics education.

Several different movements have already left their mark on mathematics education during the twentieth century, some running concurrently and others as a reaction to a different point of view. Teachers in today's schools, educated in different places and at different times, frequently continue to reflect the emphases of these various movements.

Early in this century, problems in arithmetic books were of the type that were better suited to the social needs of the adult population and did not include the absurd problems found in texts in previous decades. On the other hand, students were expected to approximate 100 percent accuracy. Drill was no longer valued for "training of the brain," but it was valued as the means of causing the child to think in terms of his capabilities.

As time went on there was more of an effort to restrict problems in arithmetic to those encountered in the normal daily lives of the adult population. It was felt in general that the school should think of arithmetic somewhat beyond the present actual needs of children, and not necessarily beyond the needs of adults. This procedure, known as the *social utility theory* was greatly extended as research on the actual use of arithmetic began. Some of the advocates of social utility theory believed that with the program simplified, results should be much better and 100 percent mastery of the fundamentals should be expected.

The emphasis on social utility resulted in the development of problem units for the different grades. For example, "A grocery store at school" in grade two, "The home garden, does it pay?" in grade four, and so on. Children studying arithmetic under the influence of social utility theory were not usually without drill exercises in the course of their progress through the grades, but arithmetic *was* understood to be something that would be used, and instruction often involved more informal pupil participation. (It is interesting to note that it was about this time — the late 1930s — that the use of games to teach arithmetic began to be encouraged).

Before long, drill came to be emphasized less, for it was thought that mastery required less drill if learning occurred in a meaningful situation; thus, there came into being the *meaning theory*. This meant that there was a movement away from stressing only social meanings toward more of a stress on mathematical meanings. The term *meaning theory* is commonly associated with this movement, which had considerable impact on instruction in the 1940s and 1950s. It was reasoned that stress on socially useful arithmetic had too often been accompanied with rote instruction on the fundamentals and by drill, which made little mathematical sense to the child. Educators who promoted meaning theory stressed the need for helping children *understand* processes, and they taught that drill was to be used only to reinforce material the child already understood.

Over the years, the word *meaningful* has been used in so many different ways that confusion has understandably resulted. When the term is used to refer to instruction in which the mathematics makes sense to the child, that is, when he understands *why*, then it is appropriate to contrast meaningful instruction with rote instruction. However, since the 1930s meaningful instruction has often been contrasted with drill or practice. As a result, dangerously little practice has been included in some programs.

Changes in elementary school mathematics programs since the mid-1950s have been rather dramatic. These changes can be viewed as an acceleration of the changes toward more mathematically meaningful instruction that had taken place during the previous two decades, perhaps with a change of focus. Several factors converged to help bring about the "revolution" that occurred.

First of all, mathematics itself had changed, and attempts to unify mathematical concepts led to new basic structures that had not yet been reflected in mathematics instruction below the university level. Another contributing factor was the accumulating information about how children learn, for it was becoming well established that children *could* learn quite complex concepts, often at a younger age. Other factors often cited include the concern that the mathematics curriculum was largely the result of historical development rather than logical development, the increasing need for an understanding of mathematics by people in business and industry, and a belief on the part of many people that there was an overemphasis on computational skills.

The elementary school mathematics programs that were developed during the late 1950s and the 1960s focused heavily upon concepts and principles and became immediately known as the *new math*. The content of programs for elementary school children contained more algebraic ideas and more geometry than had been included in previous years. In addition, such things as relationships between operations were stressed.

When the *new math* was introduced into the American educational system it was probably one of the greatest upheavals in curriculum content and procedures in modern times. It also became the victim of much ridicule by educators and layman alike. One night club entertainer was prompted to describe the purpose of *new math* "to get the idea, *rather* than the right answer." One of the authors' own mathematician friends, in comparing the *old math* with the *new math*, inferred that in the *old math* "they knew how to do it but didn't know what they were doing." whereas in the *new math*, "they know what they are doing but they don't know how to do it."

In general, the *new math* was intended to do away with a process that had focused upon rote memory and meaningless computation. Further, it was expected that the new process would make it easier for students to develop mathematical understandings. The extent to which the *new math* has achieved success has been challenged by some parents and by some educators as well. Obviously, most educational innovations have rightly been criticized when one gives consideration to the extremes that are possible in any educational process. Because of this, it now appears that attempts are being made to reach some sort of happy medium. While it is not likely that anyone wishes to revert entirely to the *old math*, at the same time, it would be desirable to avoid some of the extremes that have brought harsh criticisms of the *new math*.

At the present time this seems to be the prevailing notion among many mathematics educators. It appears that present approaches to mathematics programs for children are such that they are being directed toward situations that are more suited to the everyday facts of life. It is the premise of the present authors that the active play approach to learning about mathematics not only deals with the everyday facts of life, *but with life itself* — at least as far as the child is concerned.

MATHEMATICS READINESS

In the last chapter in our discussion of reading readiness it was indicated that it is a developmental stage at which certain factors have prepared the child for learning. Mathematics readiness can be viewed in this same general manner, since children should progress through certain developmental stages before they can be expected to be successful in the area of mathematics. For example, a child is probably not ready to take on the task of addition if he has to count objects to get a sum. Likewise, if he must add to find the product of two numbers, he is not yet ready for multiplication. Therefore, it seems that for the child to achieve mathematics readiness, time should be allowed for maturation of mental abilities and stimulation through experience. It might be said that *experience* is the key to the degree of mathematics readiness a child has attained upon entering school. In fact, research consistently shows that experience is a very important factor in readiness for learning in mathematics. It should be obvious that most of this experience will be the result of efforts of parents and others (siblings and relatives) in the home situation.

Because of experiences in mathematics — or lack thereof — children entering first grade vary a great deal in the amount of mathematical learnings they bring with them. It is becoming a common practice in many schools for teachers to try to determine how *ready* children are to deal with mathematics as they begin first grade. This gives the teacher an idea of the needs of the children and consequently serves as a basis for the teacher to group children with regard to instruction.

To give the reader some idea of how a teacher might proceed, several *diagnostic* items in the area of mathematics are given here. (It should be clearly understood that these are not standard procedures, but merely representative examples of what teachers might do to help them determine how well acquainted the children are with some of the mathematical experiences that will be dealt with as they begin their formal education.)

Ordinarily, these items are administered orally with small groups of children. The teacher tries to observe certain behavior responses of children such as hesitation in answering, inattention, lack of ability in following directions, or anything that could be interpreted as immature thinking.

Generally speaking, teachers are concerned specifically with such features as counting, number symbols, number order, ordinal use of numbers, understanding of the simple fraction of 1/2, recognition of coins, and quantitative thinking.

The teacher might try to diagnose ability in *counting* by having children respond to such questions as the following: Can anyone count to find how many boys there are in our class? Can anyone count to find out how many windows there are in our room? Can anyone tell us how many chairs we have? Can anyone tell how many pictures we have in our room? The teacher observes those children who volunteer and how correct their responses are. Different children are given an opportunity to answer the questions, and each time the responses are observed by the teacher.

In the area of *number symbols,* a teacher might use a procedure like the following. Ten cards with each card having a number (1 to 10) are placed on the chalkboard tray. The teacher then asks questions such as: Who can find the card that tells us how many ears we have? What is the number? Who can find the card that tells us how many arms we have? What is the number? Which card tells us how many fingers we have on one hand? What is the number? Which card tells us how many doors there are in our room? What is the number?

In checking the children for their knowledge of *number order,* the same procedure is followed except that the cards numbers are out of order. Such questions as the following may be asked: Can you help me put these cards back in order? Another procedure used is to ask questions such as: What number comes after 3? after 6? after 4? What is the number that comes right before 7? before 10? before 5? What is the number that comes between 1 and 3? between 6 and 8?

We mentioned in Chapter 3 that *ordinal* numbers are used to show order or succession such as first, second, and so on. This can be diagnosed by placing number cards from 1 to 6 in order along the chalkboard tray. The teacher then may ask: "Who can tell me the *first* card? the *fifth* card? the *third* card?"

To help to determine how well the children understand the concept of one-half, the teacher can use six equal sized glasses. One glass can be full, one can be empty, and the rest of the glasses can be one-fourth full, one-third full, one-half full, and three-fourths full. Such questions as the following can be asked: Who can tell me which glass if full? Who can tell me which glass is empty? Who can tell me which glass is half full? Who can tell me if there is a glass that is less than one-half full? Can you find a glass that is more than one-half full?

In diagnosing children's knowledge about *coins* the teacher will probably have ten pennies, one nickle, and one dime. The teacher holds up each of the coins to see if the children can identify them. Such questions as the following can be asked: Does a penny buy less than a nickel? Does a dime buy more than a nickel? Which buys more, a penny or a dime? Would you give a nickel for four pennies? Would you give a dime for eight pennies?

Our reason for presenting the above information is to give the reader an opportunity to see just what might be expected of a child in terms of mathematical understandings upon entering school. When parents have such information, they can provide experiences for children that will improve upon their mathematics readiness. Many of the active play experiences involving mathematics that are explained in the following sections of this chapter can be used to improve upon the child's mathematics readiness. Others are useful in helping a child with mathematics once he has started to school.

ACTIVE PLAY EXPERIENCES INVOLVING NUMBERS

When we use the term *number system* we are referring to the base ten system of numeration (by tens, hundreds, thousands, and so on). Children first need to learn the meaning of 1, 2, 3, 4, 5, 6, 7, 8, and 9. Then they learn that there is a way of using these same numbers over and over again, with zero, to describe any number, regardless of how large it might be.

Catch A Bird Alive

This is a good activity for rote* counting, 1-10. The parent and child stand side by side on a starting line. They recite the following verse:

1, 2, 3, 4, 5
I caught a bird alive;
6, 7, 8, 9, 10,
I let him go again.

The parent and child count together, and as they count 1-5 they can take jumps forward. As they say the next phrase they pretend to catch a bird in their hands. They jump back to the original starting line as they count 6-10. As they say the last phrase they pretend to let the bird go.

In this activity the child gains skill in reciting the number names 1-10 in order, an essential skill in a child's early experiences with arithmetic.

Watch the Numeral

On large sheets of paper write the numerals 1, 2, 3, 4, 5, and 6, one numeral per sheet. Be sure to make the numerals large enough so that the child can read them while moving around the room. The child starts the activity by moving around the room. The movement can be running, hopping, etc. The parent holds up a paper with one of the numerals on it. If the numeral is two, the child moves to that numeral and stands on it. The activity can continue in this manner with the parent and child changing places frequently.

This activity will help the child gain skill in recognizing the numerals 1-6. This can be helpful to the child when he begins to write numbers. Many times at about age five a child will write numbers backwards. Six year olds may also do this at

---

*Rote counting means counting from memory and rational counting means using reasoning when counting.

times; however, children by the age of seven are less likely to do so. Number recognition thus becomes important for writing numbers in the correct way.

Number Man

This activity requires four or more players; however, *the child* can be the principal player. One player, the Number Man, faces the others, who are standing on a line at the end of a playing area. These players have counted off, starting with number 1, and each has a number. In the early stages of the activity it is a good idea to have the parent play the part of the Number Man. The Number Man calls out "all numbers greater than _____." The players who have numbers greater than the one called must try to get to the other side of the playing area without being tagged by the Number Man. The Number Man may also call out "all numbers less than _____," "all even numbers," or "all odd numbers." Anyone who is tagged must help the Number Man tag the runners. Any child who runs out of turn is considered tagged.

In this activity a child can gain skill with number sequence while identifying numbers that are greater or less than a given number. When the players are lined up in sequence, it can be observed that the sets of odd numbers and even numbers involve every other whole number.

Call and Catch

This activity requires four or more players, but again the child is the principal player whom the parent observes. The players stand in a circle, and each player is assigned a different number. The parent throws a large rubber ball into the air and calls out a number by saying "Just before four" or "Next after three." For example, if the parent calls "Next after three," the player assigned the number four tries to catch the ball after it bounces.

In this activity a child can gain skill in using numbers in sequence. The parent can help a child succeed in retrieving the ball by holding it momentarily after the number is called. As a child gains more mastery of the skill the ball can be tossed up at the same time the call is made.

Red Light

This activity is a version of the one by the same name that was described in Chapter Four. The parent is *It* and stands a distance away from the child with his or her back to the child. The parent counts loudly, "10, 20, 30, 40, 50, 60, 70, 80, 90, 100, "Red Light." The child advances toward the goal line as the parent counts, but the child must stop when the parent calls "Red Light." As the parent calls "Red Light" he or she turns, and if the child is moving he must return back to the starting line. The object of the activity is to see how long it takes the child to reach the goal line. The parent and child should change places so that the child has a chance to be *It*.

This activity provides an opportunity for practice in counting by tens. The child has to anticipate the position of 100 in the sequence so as not to be caught off guard.

Postman

This activity requires four or more players who are divided into two groups. Members of one group are the postmen and are given envelopes, each having a house number written on it. Members of the other group represent the houses and hold numeral cards in their hands. Each postman runs to the various houses trying to find the correct address so he can deliver his envelope. Also, each postman must be able to read the numerals aloud. When all the letters have been delivered to the houses, the groups exchange places. The group that delivers the mail in the shortest period of time can be declared the winner.

This is a reinforcement activity that helps a child read numerals above 100 quickly. The activity can be varied by using numerals that the parent wishes to have the child practice reading.

Come With Me

This activity requires several players who stand close together in a circle. The child is *It,* and he goes around the outside of the circle. *It* taps a player and says "Come with Me." That player follows *It. It* continues in the same manner, tapping players who then follow *It* as he goes around the outside of the circle. At any time *It* may call "Go Home!" All the players following *It* run to find vacant places in the circle. The remaining player can be *It* when the activity continues. At the beginning the parent has the child count how many there are. *It* can count the players as he taps them. All the players can also count as *It* taps the players. The number of players not tapped might also be counted.

The child, when *It,* is able to count varying-sized groups in this activity. By having the child who is *It* and the other players count as the players are tapped, he is helped to see the number names related to specific objects.

Muffin Man

This activity requires several players, who stand in a circle. While all the players sing the question of the song "Muffin Man," two players stand still in the center of the circle, where they place their hands on their hips and face each other. After the question is sung, the two players in the center clasp hands and skip around the inside of the circle as everyone sings the answer: "Two of us know the Muffin Man . . ." and so on. When they finish the answer, the two players stand in front of two new players. Everyone sings the question again, then the four players in the center clasp hands and skip around the inside of the circle as all the players sing the appropriate answer: "Four of us know the Muffin Man . . ." and so on. This procedure may be repeated for eight, sixteen and so on, depending on the size of the group. In most instances the group will be comprised of no more than eight players, although more could be accommodated.

Question: Oh, do you know the Muffin Man,

the Muffin Man, the Muffin Man?
Oh, do you know the Muffin Man
who lives in Drury Lane?
Answer: Two of us know the Muffin Man,
the Muffin Man, the Muffin Man.
Two of us know the Muffin Man
who lives in Drury Lane.

In this activity experience can be gained with successive doubling. The grouping pattern associated with base two numeration is also illustrated. The parent might write number sentences on a large piece of paper showing the doubling and both addition and multiplication number sentences. What is known as *exponential notation* could also be introduced. (This is a number placed at the upper right of another number to show how many times the number is to be multiplied by itself.)

Addition Number Sentences	Multiplication Number Sentences	Exponential Notation
$1 + 1 = 2$	$2 \times 1 = 2$	$2 = 2^1$
$2 + 2 = 4$	$2 \times 2 = 4$	$2 \times 2 = 2^2$
$4 + 4 = 8$	$2 \times 4 = 8$	$2 \times 2 \times 2 = 2^3$
$8 + 8 = 16$	$2 \times 8 = 16$	$2 \times 2 \times 2 \times 2 = 2^4$

One, Two, Button My Shoe

This activity requires a minimum of three players, but as many can play as desired. The players stand toeing a line at one end of the play area. The child is the leader and takes a position in front of the group. The group and the leader carry on the following dialogue:

Leader: One, two.
Group: Button my shoe.
Leader: Three, Four.
Group: Close the door.
Leader: Five, six.
Group: Pick up sticks.
Leader: Seven, eight.
Group: Don't be late.

On the word *late* the players who were toeing the line run and try to reach another goal line a specified distance away, without being tagged by the leader. All players tagged become helpers for the next time, and the activity can continue until all are tagged. If desired the players can act out the dialogue as they say it.

This activity gives the child practice in counting by ones and twos up to eight.

Airplane Zooming

The child jumps into the air and makes a one-quarter turn to his left. He does this three times until he has made a complete turn. The same procedure is repeated except that he turns to the right. A circle can be drawn on the surface area and divided into four parts. The child can stand in the center of the circle and jump from one quarter of the circle to the other. If desired, the parent and child can call out together, "one quarter" and so on.

This is a good activity to help the child develop an understanding of the meaning of a whole number, one-half of a number and one-fourth of a number.

ACTIVE PLAY EXPERIENCES INVOLVING ARITHMETIC OPERATIONS

Certain active play experiences can provide the child with valuable experiences with the operations of arithmetic (addition, subtraction, multiplication, and division). The energetic involvement of children in the activities that follow brings an interest and enthusiasm to the learning of arithmetic operations that many children need very much.

Being a Number

This activity requires several players, with a minimum of six. Players are given numbers of 1, 2, or 3 and dispersed around the playing area. They must remain in groups that do not add up to more than three. For example, three number 1s may be in a group, or a 1 and a 2, or a 3 alone. The players move around from one group to another and, at a given signal from the parent, check to see that the groups add up to three. A number 1 can make a three by getting together with a 2. Three number 1s can get together to make three. At the signal, if a group totals more or less than three, a point can be scored against each person in the group, provided that it seems desirable to add more interest to the activity.

This activity gives an opportunity for addition of combinations 1 to 3. Also if a group has only two at the signal the parent might ask, "How many more do you need to make three? Or, if there are four in a group the question can be "How many less do you need to make three? This brings in the idea of both addition and subtraction.

Addition Name Hunt

Pieces of cardboard with addition combinations are placed in various spots around the activity area. Each combination should be expressed in a form such as, 4 + 3, 2 + 6 and so on. There should be several pieces of cardboard with different combinations for each of the sums for two through twelve (or higher). The parent has large numeral cards for two through twelve, or for the numbers being presented. The parent says "Can you find a name for _____?" then shows a numeral card to the child. The child runs to an addition combination on the floor, which is the name for the number being shown by the parent. For example, if the parent shows "6" the child will run to the combinations 2 + 4, 5 + 1, etc. The idea is to see how quickly and correctly the child can respond.

This is a good activity to help the child improve his skill in recalling and identifying pairs of addends for a given sum, an extremely important skill for the development of problem-solving ability. The parent may wish to use the same combinations that the child may be doing in school.

Fast Facts

This activity requires several players. The players are grouped according to a specific number to be thought of as a sum. If the parent knows that in school the child has been studying pairs of addends for the number four, the players are organized into groups of four. As the activity begins, the players are lined up along a line on the activity area and clustered in their groups. Opposite each group on a parallel line is placed a marker or partition. The parent calls out "Four equals two plus two," and all the groups run to the other line. The players in a group arrange themselves so that two are on one side of the marker and two are on the other side. When all have agreed that the addition fact is correctly pictured, the parent calls out "Two plus two equals four," and all of the players run back to the starting line and form their groups again. The activity continues as the parent calls out other addition facts for the same sum. If desired, a group can be given a point for being the first to picture the two addends.

A child can develop an understanding of the meaning of addition as he associates the partitioning of a set with various pairs of addends for a given sum. As a child interprets the orally given number sentences, he becomes more comfortable with the sum placed before the equal sign. The parent should be alert to observe if the child is having difficulty including himself when counting the number in each part of the partitioned group of players.

Parts of Seven

The parent and child stand about 10 to 15 feet apart, throwing a large rubber ball back and forth to each other. After passing the ball back and forth for a short time, the parent who has the ball in hand says "Seven equals four (bounces the ball four times) and _____." The parent then tosses the ball to the child, who bounces it three times and says "three" (because 7 = 4 + 3). If the parent says "Seven equals two and _____" and bounces the ball two times, the child receives the ball and bounces it five times, and so on. When the activity is varied to show two addends for a different sum, the name of the activity should be changed to suggest the sum involved. The child should also be given the opportunity to give the original call and then bounce the ball to start the activity.

The child practices recalling pairs of addends for a given sum as he determines the missing addend. The parent can match the difficulty of specific tasks to the capability of the child, and as the child improves his ability in the skill, more difficult tasks can be used.

Addition Beanbag Throw

Five large-mouth cans are tied together and numbered from one to five. The parent and child stand behind a line about 10 feet from the targets. The parent and child each have a beanbag. Each of them throws the beanbag, trying to get it in can number five, as this is worth the most points. The parent and the child each have three tries. At the end of their turn the parent and child add up their own score to see who had the most points. If necessary the parent can assist the child with the adding of his score.

An activity of this type stimulates interest in reinforcing arithmetic skills. The activity can be done with higher numbers as the child progresses. Or, there can be concentration on a specific number. For example, if the child has been studying the set of addition and subtraction facts with four as an addend, two of the three cans can be labeled with a four.

Number Man (Variation)

Four or more players are needed for this activity. Each player is assigned a number and stands behind a line at one end of the playing area. To start with, the parent can be the Number Man. The Number Man calls out addition and subtraction problems such as "five plus six" and "twelve minus four." The players who have the number that is the answer (the missing sum or addend) for the problem must try to get past the Number Man to the line on the opposite side without being tagged. If tagged, the player must help the Number Man. As play continues, the child should be given the opportunity to be the Number Man.

In this activity reinforcement is provided for recalling missing addends and sums. This extra activity will help the child who may be having difficulty with this process in school.

Five Little Birds

Five players are required for this activity. They count off from one to five. The players all stand on a line. All players recite the verse. The player with the number being repeated "flies" to a point a short distance away. This is continued until all of the "birds" have "flown" to the given point.

Five little birdies peeping through a door,
One went in and then there were four.
Four little birdies sitting in a tree,
One fell down and then there were three.
Three little birdies looking straight at you,
One went away and then there were two.
Two little birdies sitting in the sun,
One went home and then there was one.
One little birdie left all alone,
He flew away and then there were none.

If desired the following two verses can also be used:

Five little chickadees pecking at my door,
One flew away, now there're four.
Four little chickadees very afraid of me,
One flew away, now there're three.
Three little chickadees didn't know what to do,
One flew away, now there're two.
One little chickadee hopping on the ground,
He flew away, now there're none around.

In this verse they do not "fly" but move like bunnies.

Five little bunnies hopping on the floor,
One hops away and then there are four.
Four little bunnies sitting near a tree,
One hops away and then there are three.
Three little bunnies looking at you,
One hops away and then there are two.
One little bunny left all alone,
He hops away and then there are none.
All the little bunnies happy and gay,
All the little bunnies hop away.

As a child participates in this activity he dramatizes and acts out the concept of *one less than*. This method of introducing this concept to young children has been found to be much more effective than trying to verbalize it to them.

Twice as Many

This activity requires several players who stand on a line near the end of the activity area. To begin with, the parent can be the caller, who stands at the finish line 25 to 50 feet away. The caller gives directions such as "Take two hops. Now take twice as many. Take three small steps. Now take twice as many." Directions are varied in number and type of movement. Each direction is followed by "Now take twice as many." The first player to reach the finish line calls out "Twice as many," and everyone runs back to the starting line. The caller tags all those he or she can before they reach the starting line. All those tagged help the caller for the next time.

The child is able to apply his knowledge of multiplication facts for the factor two in a highly motivating activity. The parent may find that the child who is the principal player may need help to act out the called for multiplication fact. The parent may also want to check each time a new direction is given to be sure the child has multiplied by two accurately and has the correct answer.

Back to Back

Several partners stand back to back with arms interlocked at the elbows. The parent points to each group and, with the help of the players, counts by twos. If one player is left over, the number one is added and the total number of players is thereby determined. The parent calls for any size group, and on a signal the players let go and regroup themselves in groups of the size called for. If the parent calls for a group of two, the players must find a new partner. Each time the players are regrouped, they count by twos, threes, or whatever is appropriate, and add the number of players left over. (If the resulting number is not the total number of players, there has been an error, and groups should be counted again.) Whenever the number called for is larger than the group already formed, the parent may choose to ask how many players are needed for each group to become the size group that has just been called for. Whatever the size group called for, the players must hook up back to back in groups of that number. A time limit may be set. The players who are left over may rejoin the group each time there is a call to regroup.

This activity not only provides experience with the multiples of a given factor but also informally prepares a child for uneven division. In fact, he may want to predict the number of players who will be left over before the signal to start regrouping is given. The parent may choose to write number sentences to record each regrouping. For example, if there are nine players and groups of two have been called for, the record should show that four twos and one is nine or $(4 \times 2) + 1 = 9$.

Birds Fly South

Play begins with several players distributed randomly behind a starting line. The number of players is the dividend (or product). The parent gives the signal to play by calling "Birds fly south in flocks of three" (or the largest divisor that will be used). The players run to another line that has been designated as "South." At this point the players should be grouped in threes. After observing the number of flocks (the quotient), the players who remain (that is, those who were not able to be included in one of the flocks) become hawks, who take their places between the two lines. Then with the call "Scatter! The hawks are coming!" the players run back to the other line, with the hawks attempting to tag them. Note is taken of who is tagged. Play continues, with the players taking their place behind the starting line. The parent then uses the next lower number for the call. If three was used first, two would be called next. "Birds fly south in flocks of two." This continues until groups of two have been formed and they return to the starting line. Each time the number of flocks that are formed should be observed.

This activity is concerned with the meaning of division and the effect of increasing or decreasing the divisor. At the end of the activity the parent should consider the arithmetic that has been applied. If possible, the parent can record division number sentences showing the number of flocks formed when different divisors were used for the same dividend. A child should be helped to form the generalization that, for a given dividend (product), when the divisor (known factor) decreases, the quotient (unknown factor) increases in value. After this pattern is established, the number called can be reversed, beginning with the smallest divisor and working up to the highest divisor to be used. Here, the opposite of the previous statement can be developed.

Take Away, Take Away

This rhythmic activity requires a minimum of five players who stand in a circle. The child who is the principal player can be *It*. He walks around the inside of the circle. As the players sing the following song, to the tune of "Twinkle Twinkle Little Star," they act out the words of the song.

Take away, take away, take away one,
Come with me and have some fun.
Take away, take away, take away two
Come with me, oh yes please do.
Take away, take away, take away three.
All please come and skip with me.

It taps one player. This player follows behind *It*. *It* then taps a second and third player. At the end of the song all three players try to get back to their places in the circle. *It* also tries to get into one of the vacant places. The remaining player can be *It* for next time.

This activity enables a child to see demonstrated the concept of subtraction. The parent may have a child identify how many players are left each time *It* takes away one player.

Dance Around the Ring

This rhythmic activity requires nine players. Three of the players stand together. Then three more players stand together. Finally, the last three players stand together so that groups of three can be distinguished. The nine players all join hands and make a ring (circle). They sing this song to the tune of "Rock-A-Bye-Baby."

If you take three and add on three more
You will have six you know I am sure.
Again you add three and now you will find
That with these three threes you now have nine.

The song is sung through three times. When it is sung the first time the players walk around the ring. When it is sung the second time they walk into the center of the ring and back. The third time the song is sung they skip around the ring. The players are asked to think about the numbers as they do the activity.

This activity involves the idea that multiplication is a short way to add. It also provides an understanding that there can be *sets* of something, in this case sets of three people. The multiplication concept can be developed with the principal child or children as three groups of three are seen; that is, three threes make nine. As the players get together it can be pointed out that they make a group of three.

ACTIVE PLAY EXPERIENCES INVOLVING OTHER AREAS OF MATHEMATICS

Thus far, number, numeration, and the operations of arithmetic have been the mathematical concepts and skills that we have related to learning through active play. We now turn our attention to various other areas of mathematical learnings that children can come to understand through this medium. These involve geometric figures, linear and liquid measurement, telling time, and recognition of coins and their values.

It is interesting to note that one of these areas — that which is concerned with learning about basic geometric patterns — can be beneficial to the child in other educational pursuits as well as mathematics. This is concerned with the child's beginning efforts to learning to write. As will be seen in the following chapter, beginning writing experiences involve circles, parts of circles, and straight lines, which of course, are geometric figures.

Show a Shape

The child stands a short distance away from the parent, who calls, "Take two turns and show a _____," specifying the two-dimensional geometric figure the child is to form with his arms or body. The child turns around twice, then forms the figure named. For example, a circle can be suggested easily with both arms overhead as hands touch. By bending elbows but keeping hands and forearms rigid, different quadrilaterals can be formed. A child who touches his toes while keeping his legs straight makes a triangle. At times the parent and child can work together to form other figures.

Lines, line segments, rays, and angles can also be shown. A child can let his extended arms represent a part of a line, with a fist used to suggest the end point. An infinite extension can be suggested by pointing the finger. For angles, the torso can become the vertex as the arms are swung to different positions. Acute, right, and obtuse angles can all be pictured in this way. Of course, a child without previous experience will need to be given instructions in the movement before the activity is played.

This activity can help a child learn that geometric figures are not just marks on paper, that they consist of a set of locations in space. The activity can be used to introduce selected definitions, for example, an obtuse angle. However, because many of the figures formed will be suggestive rather than precise, the activity will usually be used for reinforcement.

Triangle Run

A large triangle is marked off on the activity area with a base at each vertex. (This is like a triangle baseball area instead of a square area.) The child positions himself on any one of the bases. On a signal the child leaves the base he is standing on and runs to his right around the triangle, touching each base on the way. The idea is for the child to see how fast he can get around the bases.

This activity helps to demonstrate certain properties of a triangle, for example, the three angles. It is best to mark off differently shaped triangles from time to time so that the properties observed can be generalized to all triangles.

Jump the Shot

This activity was described in Chapter Five, but it is repeated here for convenience. The parent holds a length of rope with an object tied to one end. The object should be something soft such as a yarn ball or a beanbag. The parent starts by swinging the rope around in a circle close to the feet of the child and slightly above the surface area. The child attempts to avoid being hit by the object by jumping over it when it goes by. With several players a circle can be formed with the parent in the center of the circle, and the same procedure is used.

This activity can be used to help the child visualize not only the circle itself but the radius of a circle as well. The child should be helped to understand that the rope, which represents the radius, is the same length from the center to any point along the circle.

Run Circle Run

This activity requires several players, who form a circle by holding hands and facing inward. Depending on the size of the group, players count off by twos or threes (for small groups) or fours, fives, or sixes (for large groups). The parent calls one of the assigned numbers. All of the players with that number start running around the circle in a specified direction; each runner tries to tag one or more players running in front of him. As a successful runner reaches his starting point without being tagged, he stops. Runners who are tagged go to the interior of the circle. Another number is called, and the same procedure is followed. This continues until all have been called. The circle is reformed, new numbers are assigned to the players, and the activity is repeated. As the number of players deceases, a smaller circle can be drawn on the surface area inside the larger circle; the players must stay out of the smaller circle when running around to their places.

This activity deals with the concept that a circle is a simple, closed curve, and also the interior of a circle. The parent should help a child note that when the players form a circle by holding hands, they make a continuous, simple, closed shape. As they do the activity it can be observed what happens to the size of the circle as parts of it break off. It can also be learned that the space within the circle is called the interior of the circle.

Three Bounce

The child stands behind a starting line. A small circle about 1 foot in diameter is drawn about 15 feet in front of the starting line. At a signal from the parent the child runs with a ball to the circle. At the circle he attempts to bounce the ball three times within the circle, that is, in the interior of the circle. If the ball at any time does not land on the interior, the child must start over from the starting line. When the child has bounced the ball three times within the circle, he returns to the starting line. The idea is to see how long it takes the child to complete the activity.

If several players are used for this activity, they form into groups and make rows behind the starting line. The same procedure is used but the activity is done in relay fashion, with a circle drawn in front of each relay team. The first player attempts to bounce thé ball in the circle; when finished, he returns to the starting line and touches the next player, who does the same thing. The first relay team to finish is the winner.

This activity concentrates on the concept of the interior of a figure. The word *interior* is stressed in explaining the activity. A child can thus learn the meaning of this term by practical use. However, so that a child does not associate the term only with circular regions, other geometric shapes such as triangles and squares can be drawn from time to time.

Inside Out

Several players can be involved in this activity. They divide into groups of four or more. Players on each group join hands to form a circle in which each player faces toward the inside. When the parent calls "inside out," each group tries to turn its circle inside out; that is, while *continuing* to hold hands, the players move so as to face out instead of in. To do this, a player will have to lead his group under the joined hands of two group members. The first group to complete a circle with players facing toward the outside of the circle can be declared the winner.

This activity is designed as a kind of puzzle or problem-solving activity, for the goal is presented to the players and they are not told how it is possible to turn the circle inside out. It is designed to be the initial encounter with the process involved.

Ring Toss

A regular, inexpensive ring toss game can be used for this activity, and a meter stick or a yardstick is also required. The parent and the child each have a ring. One post is used for both the parent and the child. Either the child or parent takes the first turn in tossing his or her ring. Then each takes the measuring stick and measures the distance between the post and the ring, provided that the ring did not "ring" the post. The player whose ring is closest scores a point. Before starting the activity, the parent should indicate how precisely measurements are to be made. For example, if the meter stick is used, measurements will probably be to the nearest centimeter. If a yardstick is used, the nearest quarter-inch might be specified.

This activity provides the child with an opportunity to develop his measuring skills. He will get additional practice if he checks the parent's ring.

Add-A-Jump

The parent and the child serve as their own scorekeeper. They both stand on a starting line. The child steps on the starting line and jumps as far as he can. The parent does likewise. The parent marks where the child landed, and the child marks where the parent landed. Each then measures the distance he or she jumped. If desired, several jumps can be taken by each, and the distance of all jumps can be added.

This activity can use linear measurement, figuring an average or means, and addition, including decimals. In addition to developing measuring skills, this activity provides practice and experience in comparing distances. Either English or metric units can be used for measuring. If the child is studying this in school, he could measure in meters and express the distance with a decimal including tenths and hundredths (to the nearest centimeter). An average or mean can be determined by adding the distance of all jumps and dividing by the number of jumps.

Beanbag Throw

The parent and child both stand on a starting line, with each having a beanbag. The child tosses the beanbag from his starting line and the parent does likewise. The parent marks the spot where the child's beanbag landed, and the child marks the spot where the parent's beanbag landed. Each measures his or her own throw with a tape measure. Each takes three throws and adds all of the throws to determine the total distance.

By doing his own computing the child can determine what an average is and how to find an average; therefore, it is best to have the child compute his own average. The activity can also provide practice in measuring, adding, and dividing. The parent should give assistance to the child as needed.

Milkman Tag

This activity requires several players. Two groups of three milkmen are selected and given milk truck bases. One group might be called Chocolate, the other White. The remaining players are called Pints. On a given signal, one milkman from each group tries to tag any of the Pints. When he tags one they both go to the milk truck, and another milkman goes after a Pint. The parent sets a goal of so many quarts to be gained to win. The players must figure out how many Pints will be needed to make the necessary number of quarts.

A child is provided with a highly motivating activity for applying the idea of liquid measurement that 2 pints are equivalent to 1 quart. Players may want to group Pints in twos to determine how many quarts each group has.

Tick Tock

Several players form a circle that represents a clock. Two players are runners, and they are called Hour and Minute. The players chant, "What time is it?" Minute then chooses the hour and calls it out (six o'clock). Hour and Minute must stand still while the players in the circle call "One o'clock, two o'clock, three o'clock, four o'clock, five o'clock, six o'clock (or whatever time has been chosen). When the players get to the chosen hour, the chase begins. Hour chases Minute clockwise around the outside of the circle. If Hour can catch Minute before the players in the circle once again call out "One o'clock, two o'clock, etc." (the same hour as counted the first time), he chooses another player to become Hour. The activity can also be played counting by half-hours.

A child not only gets practice in calling the hours in order but he also gains experience with the concept of the term *clockwise*.

Double Circle

Several players are arranged in a double circle. The outside circle has one more player than the inside circle. The players in both circles skip around to their right (each circle goes in the opposite direction) until a signal is given to stop. Each player then tries to find a partner from the other circle. The player left without a partner is said to be "in the doghouse." Play can continue as long as desired.

This activity is good to develop the idea of time-telling terminology — clockwise and counter clockwise.

Midnight

The child is the chaser, and he goes to a designated line a given distance away with his back turned to the parent. The parent stands on a starting line and then approaches the child.

As the parent approaches the child, he or she asks the child what time it is. The child can give any time he wishes, such as eight o'clock, eleven o'clock, and etc. If he says "midnight" the parent runs back to the starting line, and the child attempts to tag the parent. The parent and child change positions and the activity can continue. If desired, several players can engage in this activity. This activity gives the child an opportunity to practice telling time by hours.

Cobbler, Cobbler

Several players form a circle, with one player in the center. The player in the center holds an object that is supposed to represent a shoe. As the following verse is recited, the player in the center passes the "shoe" to another in the circle.

Cobbler, cobbler
Mend my shoe.
Have it done by
Half-past two.

The shoe is then passed behind the backs of the players during the reciting of the next verse, which is as follows:

Sew it up or
Sew it down.
Now see with whom
The shoe is found.

On the word "found" the player who has the shoe becomes *It* and goes to the center of the circle.

This activity can develop an understanding of telling time by the half-hour. The players may make up other verses, using other half-hour intervals, such as half-past three, half-past four, and so on.

Stepping Stones

On the activity area, draw a stream with stepping stones arranged so that the child can take different paths across the stream. Place a coin on each stepping stone. Caution the child not to fall in the stream by making a mistake naming the coins. As the child chooses a stepping stone to cross the stream and steps on the stone, he must name the coin and its value. It is important to change coins frequently. The parent may wish to do the activity first so as to help the child in his recognition of the coins.

This activity provides an interesting situation for a child to practice naming coins and stating their values.

Bank

This activity can be conducted with a small number of players, and even two players could do the activity if desired. The child is selected to be the Bank. The rest of the players stand at a starting line about 20 feet away from the Bank. Bank calls out the number of pennies, nickels, or dimes a player may take. (A penny is one small step, a nickel equals five penny steps, and a dime equals ten penny steps; hopping and jumping can also be used instead of steps.) Bank calls a player's name and says "George, take three pennies." George must answer "May I?" Then Bank says "Yes, you may" or "No, you may not." If George forgets to say "May I?" he must return to the starting line. The first player to reach the Bank becomes the Bank for the next time. All players should have a chance to be the Bank.

By taking the steps forward toward the Bank, a child can gain an understanding that a nickel has the same value as five pennies and a dime has the same value as ten pennies.

Banker and the Coins

This activity requires several players; each is given a sign to wear, which denotes one of the following: five cents, ten cents, twenty-five cents, fifty cents, nickel, dime, quarter, or half-dollar. To start the activity the child can be the Banker. He calls out different amounts of money up to one dollar. The players run and group themselves with the other players until their group totals the amount of money called by the Banker. All players should have a chance to be the Banker.

A child can gain practice in combining different amounts of

money to arrive at a specific amount. He can learn that there are usually several different ways one can combine coins to produce a specified amount of money. As the parent checks that a group is correct, he or she can have the whole group count it out. In this way, a child will be more likely to learn about values of coins if he is unsure.

THE MATHEMATICS ACTIVE PLAY STORY

The widespread success resulting from the use of active play reading content reported in the previous chapter inspired the development of the same general type of reading content that would also include mathematics experiences. This kind of reading content was arbitrarily called *the mathematics active play story.*

Early attempts to develop mathematics active play stories were patterned after the original procedure used in providing for active play reading content: that is several stories were written around active play experiences, the only difference being that the content also involved reference to mathematics experiences. These stories were tried out in a number of situations. It soon became apparent that with some children the understanding of the mathematics concepts in the story was too difficult. The reason for this appeared to be that certain children could not handle the task of reading while at the same time developing an understanding of the mathematics aspect of the story. It was then decided that since *listening* is a first step in learning to read, auditory input should be used. This procedure involved having a child or children listen to a story, perform the activity, and simultaneously try to develop the mathematics concept. When it appeared desirable, this process was extended by having a child try to read the story after having engaged in the activity. Thus, our first recommendation would be to have the parent simply read the story to the child. If it seems practical under the particular circumstances, then the APAV technique referred to in *Chapter Five* could be used.

Several experiments with the mathematics active play story have shown somewhat conclusively that children can benefit from this listening experience and develop the mathematics concept in the story as well. The following discussion is an example of an experiment of this approach with a group of thirty children. The name of the story is "Find a Friend," and it is an adaptation of the activity "Busy Bee" that was presented in Chapter Four. The mathematics concepts in this story are *groups or sets of two; counting by twos; and beginning concepts of multiplication.*

FIND A FRIEND

IN THIS GAME EACH CHILD FINDS A FRIEND.

STAND BESIDE YOUR FRIEND.

YOU AND YOUR FRIEND MAKE A GROUP OF TWO.

ONE CHILD IS *IT*.

HE DOES NOT STAND BESIDE A FRIEND.

HE CALLS "MOVE!"

ALL FRIENDS FIND A NEW FRIEND.

IT TRIES TO FIND A FRIEND.

THE CHILD WHO DOES NOT FIND A FRIEND IS *IT*.

PLAY THE GAME.

COUNT THE NUMBER OF FRIENDS STANDING TOGETHER.

COUNT BY TWO.

SAY "TWO, FOUR, SIX."

COUNT ALL THE GROUPS THIS WAY.

The group of first grade children with which this experiment was conducted bordered on the remedial level (slow learners) and had no previous experience in counting by twos. Before the activity, each child was checked for the ability. Also, the children had no previous classroom experience with beginning concepts of multiplication.

The story was read to the children and the directions were discussed. The game was demonstrated by the experimenter and several children. Five pairs of children were used at one time. As the game was being played, the activity was stopped momentarily, and the child who was *It* at that moment was asked to count the groups by twos. The participants were then changed, the number participating changed, and the activity was repeated.

In evaluating the experiment it was found that this was a very successful experience from a learning standpoint. Before the activity, none of the children were able to count by twos. A check following the activity showed that eighteen of the thirty children who participated were able to count rationally to ten by twos. Seven of the children were able to count rationally to six, and two were able to count to four. Three children showed no understanding of the concept. No attempt was made to check beyond ten because in playing the game the players were limited to numbers under ten.

There appeared to be a significant number of children who had profited from this experience in a very short period of time. The teacher of the group maintained that in a more conventional teaching situation, the introduction and development of this concept with children at this low level of ability would have taken a great deal more teaching time, and the results would have been attained at a much slower rate.

Following are several mathematics active play stories that the parent can use. The story should be read to the child or group, as the case may be, and then the directions of the story are discussed. This is followed by participation in the activity with an attempt being made to develop an understanding of the mathematics concept(s) in the story. Each story is accompanied with an identification of the concepts along with suggestions as to how the concepts might be developed.

JUMP AWAY

IN THIS GAME CHILDREN JUMP.

SIX PLAYERS STAND IN A LINE.*

ONE PLAYER JUMPS AWAY.

NOW THERE ARE FIVE PLAYERS.

ANOTHER JUMPS AWAY.

NOW THERE ARE FOUR.

ANOTHER JUMPS AWAY.

NOW THERE ARE THREE.

ANOTHER JUMPS AWAY.

NOW THERE ARE TWO.

ANOTHER JUMPS AWAY.

NOW THERE IS ONE.

THAT PLAYER JUMPS AWAY.

NOW ALL HAVE JUMPED AWAY.

Mathematics Skills and Concepts
Subtraction through six
Taking away one
Geometric figure (line)
Suggestions for the Parent
1. The parent can call attention that the players are standing in a line. A line could be drawn to help in the understanding of this geometric figure.
2. The parent can ask the player who jumps away to call out how many there are left as he jumps, or after he jumps. If he does not know he can turn around and count the number.
3. The parent may wish to put the subtraction facts through six on flash cards and use them in connection with the activity. This might be an evaluative technique for a child after participation in the activity.

---

*fewer if six are not available

JUMP AND TURN

STAND STRAIGHT.

PUT YOUR FEET TOGETHER.

JUMP UP.

TURN AS YOU JUMP.

NOW YOU ARE LOOKING THE OTHER WAY.

YOU ARE HALFWAY AROUND.

JUMP AGAIN.

NOW YOU ARE BACK AGAIN.

YOU ARE ALL THE WAY AROUND.

YOU JUMPED AROUND.

YOU TOOK TWO JUMPS.

Mathematics Skills and Concepts
Vocabulary (half and whole)
Addition of fractions (two halves make a whole)
Suggestions for the Parent
1. The parent can show the child that he made two jumps to get the "whole" way around.
2. Two half circles can be drawn on the surface area or made out of cardboard as an example of two halves. When the child takes the first jump he has made the first half circle and with the second jump the second half, making the whole circle.

HOP AND JUMP

STAND STRAIGHT.

NOW STAND ON ONE FOOT.

HOP ON THIS FOOT.

HOP AGAIN.

NOW STAND ON BOTH FEET.

JUMP ON BOTH FEET.

JUMP FOUR TIMES.

TELL HOW MANY TIMES YOU HOPPED.

TELL HOW MANY TIMES YOU JUMPED.

TELL HOW MANY MORE TIMES YOU JUMPED.

TELL HOW MANY FEWER TIMES YOU HOPPED.

Mathematical Skills and Concepts
Addition
Subtraction
Rational counting
Inequality of numbers (more than, less than)
Suggestions for the Parent
1. Have the child count as he hops and jumps.
2. The activity can be repeated a number of times using different combinations.
3. For a child who may have difficulty remembering how many more or how many fewer, one footprint can be drawn on a piece of cardboard to represent a hop and two footprints can be drawn on a piece of cardboard to represent a jump. The child can be given the cardboard and he can trace his own feet.

MRS. BROWN'S MOUSE TRAP*

SOME OF THE PLAYERS STAND IN A CIRCLE.

THEY HOLD HANDS.

THEY HOLD THEM HIGH.

THIS WILL BE A MOUSE TRAP.

THE OTHER PLAYERS ARE MICE.

THEY GO IN AND OUT OF THE CIRCLE.

ONE PLAYER WILL BE MRS. BROWN.

SHE WILL SAY "SNAP!"

PLAYERS DROP HANDS.

THE MOUSE TRAP CLOSES.

SOME MICE WILL BE CAUGHT.

COUNT THEM.

TELL HOW MANY.

TELL HOW MANY WERE NOT CAUGHT.

Mathematics Skills and Concepts
Rational counting
Addition
Subtraction
Suggestions for the Parent
1. All of the players can count together the number caught.
2. All of the players can count together the number not caught.
3. If the parent wishes, the players who are caught can stand in a line facing those not caught. This way the difference can easily be seen.

---

*Gender can be changed as necessary — Mr. or Mrs. Brown.

HOP ALONG

HOP ON ONE FOOT.

NOW HOP ON THE OTHER FOOT.

HOP TWO TIMES ON YOUR LEFT FOOT.

HOP SIX TIMES ON YOUR RIGHT FOOT.

YOU HOPPED MORE TIMES ON YOUR RIGHT FOOT.

TELL HOW MANY MORE.

Mathematics Skills and Concepts
Addition
Subtraction
Rational counting
Vocabulary (left and right)
Inequality of numbers (more than)
Suggestions for the Parent
1. Have the child count as he hops.
2. The parent can put the number of hops on flash cards to show the difference.
3. Left and right footprints can be drawn on the surface area or cardboard, and if the child has difficulty with right and left he can hop on these.

RUN ACROSS

THE PLAYERS STAND IN A LINE.

THEY STAND BESIDE EACH OTHER.

ONE PLAYER IS *IT*.

THE PLAYER WHO IS *IT* GOES IN FRONT OF THE LINE.

HE CALLS "RUN!"

THE PLAYERS RUN TO THE OTHER END.

IT TAGS AS MANY AS HE CAN.

TELL HOW MANY WERE TAGGED.

TELL HOW MANY WERE LEFT.

THE PLAYERS WHO WERE TAGGED HELP *IT*.

AGAIN *IT* CALLS "RUN!"

MORE ARE TAGGED BY *IT* AND HIS HELPERS.

TELL HOW MANY WERE TAGGED.

TELL HOW MANY WERE LEFT.

PLAY UNTIL ALL BUT ONE IS TAGGED.

HE CAN BE *IT* FOR NEXT TIME.

Mathematics Skills and Concepts
Addition
Subtraction
Rational counting
Geometric figure (line)
Suggestions for the Parent
1. All the players can count together the number tagged.
2. All the players can count together the number left.
3. The players tagged can stand in a line facing those who were left. This way the difference can easily be seen.
4. The parent can call attention that they are standing on a line. A line could be drawn to help them understand the geometric figure.

MOVE LIKE A RABBIT

YOU CAN MOVE LIKE A RABBIT.

FIRST, YOU STOOP DOWN.

SECOND, YOU PUT YOUR HANDS ON THE GROUND.

THIRD, YOU JUMP LIKE A RABBIT.

MOVE LIKE A RABBIT.

SHOW AND TELL WHAT YOU DO FIRST.

SHOW AND TELL WHAT YOU DO SECOND.

SHOW AND TELL WHAT YOU DO THIRD.

MOVE AGAIN LIKE A RABBIT.

Mathematics Skills and Concepts
Ordinal numbers
Sequence of numbers
Suggestions for the Parent
1. Flash cards can be made with the ordinals *First, Second,* and *Third* on them. If the parent wishes, the flash cards can be used when the child is doing the activity.
2. The sequential order can be pointed out as the child goes through each of the three steps of the activity.
3. The parent might wish to have the child say what he does; that is, "First, I do this, Second I do this, and Third I do this."

SING AND TAP

IT TAKES SEVEN PLAYERS TO DO THIS SONG AND DANCE.

SIX OF THE PLAYERS HOLD HANDS TO MAKE A CIRCLE.

ONE PLAYER STANDS IN THE CIRCLE.

NOW EVERYONE SINGS THIS SONG.

SING IT TO THE TUNE OF "LONDON BRIDGE IS FALLING DOWN."

> ONE PLUS TWO PLUS THREE MAKE SIX.
>
> ALL MAKE SIX, ALL MAKE SIX.
>
> THREE PLUS TWO PLUS ONE MAKE SIX.
>
> MAKE SIX ALSO.

THE SIX PLAYERS WALK AROUND THE CIRCLE AS THEY SING.

THE OTHER PLAYER WALKS AROUND IN THE CIRCLE.

THE PLAYERS STOOP DOWN WHEN THE SONG ENDS.

THE PLAYER IN THE CIRCLE TRIES TO TAG SOMEONE.

HE TRIES TO TAG A PLAYER BEFORE HE GETS DOWN.

THINK OF THE NUMBERS AS YOU SING.

$1 + 2 + 3 = 6, 3 + 2 + 1 = 6.$

THINK OF HOW THEY ARE CHANGED BUT STILL MAKE SIX.

Mathematics Skills and Concepts
Commutative law (the sum is the same regardless of the order)
Addition
Suggestions for the Parent
1. To reinforce the understanding of communtative law the parent can put $1 + 2 + 3 = 6$ and $3 + 2 + 1 = 6$ on flash cards before and/or after the activity.
2. The above procedure can also be used for the addition combinations.

GO UP AND DOWN

LET'S STAND FACING EACH OTHER.

NOW LET'S HOLD HANDS.

NOW YOU STOOP DOWN.

NOW YOU STAND AND I'LL STOOP DOWN.

LET'S COUNT AS WE GO UP AND DOWN.

YOU SAY "ONE."

I'LL SAY "TWO."

LET'S GO UP AND DOWN 10 TIMES.

YOU WILL SAY "1 3, 5, 7, 9."

YOU WILL BE COUNTING BY ODD NUMBERS.

I WILL SAY "2, 4, 6, 8, 10."

I WILL BE COUNTING BY EVEN NUMBERS.

MAYBE WE WILL BE ABLE TO DO IT MORE TIMES COUNTING THE SAME WAY.

Mathematics Skills and Concepts
Odd and even numbers
Counting by twos
Suggestions for the Parent
1. After the parent and child go up and down together, the child can do it alone counting by twos as he does it.
2. The starting position can be changed so that the parent starts with one.

A STUNT WITH FOUR PARTS

HERE IS A STUNT WITH FOUR PARTS.

FIRST YOU STAND STRAIGHT WITH FEET TOGETHER.

HANDS ARE AT YOUR SIDE.

NEXT YOU STOOP DOWN TO A SQUAT POSITION.

YOUR HANDS ARE IN FRONT ON THE GROUND.

NOW YOU HAVE DONE THE FIRST PART OF THE STUNT.

YOU HAVE DONE 1/4 OF THE STUNT.

NEXT YOU KICK YOUR LEGS WAY BACK.

NOW YOU HAVE DONE 1/2 OF THE STUNT.

NEXT YOU BRING YOUR LEGS BACK TO THE SQUAT POSITION.

NOW YOU HAVE DONE 3/4 OF THE STUNT.

NOW YOU STAND UP STRAIGHT AGAIN.

NOW YOU HAVE DONE THE WHOLE STUNT.

YOU CAN DO IT AS MANY TIMES AS YOU LIKE.

Mathematics Skills and Concepts
Fractional parts of a whole (1/4, 1/2, 3/4)
Addition of fractions
Suggestions for the Parent
1. The parent can make a circle out of cardboard and cut it into fourths. As the child does each part of the stunt the fourths can be put together.
2. Another variation would be to draw a circle on the surface area. The child makes his jumps in the circle, calling out the fractional part as he jumps.

As suggested in the previous chapter, parents may want to try to develop their own original stories. The reader is referred back to the guidelines given in Chapter Five for assistance in this endeavor.

Chapter Seven

HOW TO HELP YOUR CHILD WITH WRITING THROUGH ACTIVE PLAY

IN Chapter Four we reported that it was estimated that about 75 percent of the waking hours are spent in
verbal communication, and that 9 percent of this time is spent
in writing as compared to 45 percent in listening, 30 percent in
speaking, and 16 percent in reading. Simply because only 9
percent of the waking hours are spent in expressing ourselves
through writing is no reason to minimize its importance. No
doubt the reason for this low percentage figure is that there are
far fewer opportunities to *express* ourselves in writing than in
speaking, in the same way that there are far fewer ways to
receive the thoughts and feelings of others through *reading*
than there are through *listening*. Yet, reading is considered by
many to be the most important communicative skill.

Since so little attention appears to have been given to the
basic R of writing as compared to reading and mathematics, we
feel obligated to go into some detail in this chapter about some
of the concerns of writing before getting into how to help the
child to learn to write and improve upon this ability through
active play.

Almost all children want to write, and prior to starting
school many children make an attempt. The child's desire to
write most likely comes from his feeling that he can create
something by scribbling on a piece of paper and from his
wanting to imitate. Usually between the ages of three and four
years, the young child makes marks for his name on birthday
and Christmas cards to relatives and friends. From four to six
years of age, he may try to write his name or copy a "thank-
you" note that he has dictated to a parent or older brother or
sister. At an early age children have been known, much to the
alarm of some parents, to write on the walls to express themselves. Unfortunately, too many children are punished for this
practice when they should be rewarded by being provided with

writing materials to express themselves.

For the most part, children enter first grade with a desire to write. As the child develops and grows in his ability to express his thoughts and feelings well, he moves from writing one sentence "on his own" to writing many sentences involving length and structure and the organization of ideas into paragraphs.

It should be noted that merely providing opportunities to write will not necessarily mean that children will improve their writing. Direct guidance is needed by parents and teachers. Both parents and teachers should recognize that skills should be considered as a means to an end and not necessarily ends in themselves. The important factors to consider are that (1) most all children want to write, and (2) they will perhaps write with originality, creativity, and spontaneity.

There is a high relationship between spelling and writing. To learn to spell a word the child uses the same word recognition skills that he uses in reading. As the child writes, he spells the word that he has heard (listening), has spoken (speaking), and has read (reading). These relationships make it much easier for the child to spell.

Handwriting involves physical coordination and manipulation. Thus, among other things, handwriting involves the use of muscles and bones of the hand and wrist. In addition, it is concerned with a high-level refinement between the hands and the eyes. As far as total language development is concerned, writing is preceded by listening, speaking and reading. The child develops a listening vocabulary, and he will likely try to put into oral language the words he hears. Next, he may read about things that are of interest to him, and finally he will try to put into writing those things with which he is familiar.

For the above reason, it is the general opinion that *manuscript* writing may be best suited for children at the primary school level. In this type of writing all the letters of the alphabet are formed with straight lines and circles or parts of circles. The size of the writing tends to decrease with the child's development. Although the research in this area is inconclusive, the trend appears to be much in favor of manuscript for the beginners. Children who begin their writing experiences with manuscript seem to write more freely: they use a larger number of different words than do most children who begin with the cursive form. This form (cursive) requires the joining of letters into words, and it involves varying degrees of slanting. It is also interesting to note that children who begin their school experiences with manuscript seem to spell a larger number of words correctly than do children who begin with cursive writing. Ordinarily, as the child develops, cursive writing is introduced. (Later on in the chapter we will devote a more detailed discussion to manuscript and cursive writing.)

Learning to write is a highly individualized skill. To serve its purpose as a form of communication, legible handwriting should be produced with ease and adequate speed. An important aspect is the development of what might be termed a "handwriting consciousness" or the desire to write well so that others may read it easily. Parents can be most helpful to their children in this regard.

WRITING READINESS

It is necessary for parents to have some understanding of the importance of writing readiness so that they will not unwittingly push their children into writing before they are ready for this experience.

As was the case with reading readiness and mathematics readiness, children need to progress through certain developmental stages as far as writing readiness is concerned. There appears to be a marked relationship between maturity and writing readiness because, among other things, writing is dependent upon skill in movement, manual dexterity and eye-hand coordination. Movements of the eyes tend to develop sooner than the more refined finger movements. Therefore, the former will guide the writing hand as the child begins to write. At a later time both of these movements become coordinated to the extent that writing becomes more or less an automatic process.

An important writing readiness factor for the parent to keep in mind is that it is a common characteristic for children to reverse letters, such as writing *d* for *b*. This is likely due to the limited development of eye-hand coordination previously mentioned, and it can be expected to occur in children at five or six years of age. In fact, immature development in eye-hand coordination may continue in some children until they are well beyond six years of age.

Alert teachers are sensitive to the importance of writing readiness, and ordinarily they will spend some time on readiness skills at the outset of the writing program when a child enters a school.

MANUSCRIPT AND CURSIVE WRITING

We have already mentioned the difference between manuscript and cursive writing: in manuscript writing the letters are formed by straight lines and circles or parts of circles, while cursive writing requires joined letters and the slanting of letters as well. This is an example of manuscript writing:

a b c

This is an example of cursive writing:

abc

There has long been a controversy regarding these two forms of writing. Most of this has centered around when to make the transition from manuscript to cursive writing for the average child. At one time it was thought that children might begin cursive writing at about the fourth grade. At the present time it is a more common practice to start cursive writing near the end of the second grade or at the beginning of the third grade. In some instances it is felt that manuscript writing can be eliminated altogether, and that the child should start his writing experience with cursive writing. This school of thought has become more and more pronounced among those people who deal with children with learning disabilities.

In any event, the present consensus of opinion appears to be that the average child should start with manuscript writing and then proceed to cursive writing at the proper time. This means that individual differences should be taken into account and that individual children might well be permitted to develop their own style rather than being held to any given standard.

TEACHING WRITING IN SCHOOLS

If a parent is to meet with any degree of success in his or her efforts to prepare a child for school in the area of handwriting, it is important to have some idea of writing programs in schools.

It should be recognized that there is a great variation in the educational preparation of teachers as far as the teaching of handwriting is concerned. It is possible that some teachers will have had some extensive previous educational experience in the teaching of handwriting. However, it is perhaps more likely that this will not necessarily be the case. It is entirely possible that the educational experience of some may have been limited to that which was included in a course encompassing all of the areas of language development — listening, speaking, reading, and writing. These statements should not be interpreted as an indictment against any of our teacher education institutions. It is simply that in most instances a great deal more time is directed to methods of teaching reading than to listening, speaking, and writing combined.

Although there is some variation from one school to another, the following information suggests generally what a majority of elementary schools are attempting to do in the area of handwriting.

Several years ago the Commission of the English Curriculum of the National Council of Teachers of English proposed four objectives of writing. The first of these was *ease* in writing. If a child can approach his task with confidence and a sense of adequacy, he can put his energy into making his writing serve his purpose and often find pleasure in doing it. The second objective was *clarity*, which is intimately associated with ease.

The third objective, *suitability* in writing, is highly important for all social purposes, and the fourth objective, *orginality*, adds flavor and interest for both writer and reader. In general, most elementary schools appear to be trying to reach these goals in the curriculum area of writing.

As in all school subjects, the teaching of handwriting proceeds from the less difficult to the more difficult tasks. The usual sequence of tasks involves *readiness skills, manuscript writing,* and *cursive writing.* To provide for orderly achievement of the child in handwriting, these tasks are divided in the specific skills required for each task.

Readiness Skills

Readiness skills are mainly concerned with the writing *strokes* that will eventually be used to form manuscript letters. These strokes are ordinarily taught in the following sequence:

1. Vertical lines. (The stroke is from the top to bottom.)

2. Horizontal lines. (The stroke is from left to right.)

3. Backward circle. (The stroke starts at the beginning of the arrow.)

4. Up and over half circle. (The stroke goes up and then down.)

5. Down and under half circle. (The stroke goes down and then up.)

6. Forward circle. (The stroke starts at the beginning of the arrow.)

7. Right slanting line. (The stroke starts at the top and slants to the right.)

8. Left slanting line. (The stroke starts at the top and slants to the left.)

A parent may wish to try some of these readiness strokes with the preschool child. Before asking the child to apply the strokes on paper with a crayon or large pencil, it can be useful to have the child make large strokes in the air. This can serve the purpose of having the child "get the feel" of the movement before making direct application of it with paper and pencil.

Manuscript Writing

In general, when children begin manuscript writing, paper with ruled lines is used. The reason for using lined paper is that it makes it easier for the child to form the letters. It provides the child with an opportunity to judge height relationships of letters to each other as well as the available writing space.

Some teachers feel that it may be wise to begin the writing experience with unlined paper. The main reason given for this practice is that it provides the child with a more relaxed and rhythmic pattern of writing. For example, the lower case (small letter) of l is simply a vertical stroke line, while the upper case (capital letter) of L is a vertical and horizontal stroke. This can be done easily without the use of lined paper.

The most widely used school handwriting program, which has been developed by the Zaner-Bloser Company of Columbus, Ohio, recommends the following manuscript writing sequence for children:

l L, i I, t T
o O, c C, a A, e E
r R, m M, n N, u U, s S
d D, f F, h H, b B
v V, w W, k K, x X, z Z
g G, y Y, p P, j J, q Q

Parents who would like to assist their preschool children with handwriting might want to consider this sequence rather than having the child use the traditional alphabetical order.

Cursive Writing

As previously mentioned, cursive writing differs from manuscript writing because it involves more of a slant, and the letters are joined together to form a word. After the child has become reasonably proficient in manuscript writing, under the skillful guidance of the teacher he makes the transition from manuscript to cursive writing.

Usually, the child is afforded the opportunity to view both manuscript and cursive writing to see some of the similarities and differences. Many classrooms have permanent examples of both manuscript and cursive writing on the chalkboard, and this is helpful to the child. Ordinarily, the teacher will demonstrate the slanting and joining of letters on the chalkboard to show the movement from manuscript to cursive writing. Teachers who deal with children in this stage of their writing development report that there is a great deal of eagerness on the part of children to get into cursive writing.

Handedness

Handedness of the child is not necessarily a problem for the teacher if it is detected early. If the parent is reasonably sure that the child has established a preference for the left hand before entering school, this information should be given to the teacher. Teachers themselves can identify preferred handedness by observing the hand used in certain activities.

The main factor taken into account for left-handed children is that of position. When using the chalkboard the child can stand at the left side and when seated he should also be on the left side. The purpose of this is to keep a left-handed child and a right-handed child from interfering with each other as they proceed with their writing experiences.

SOME GUIDELINES FOR PARENTS IN HELPING CHILDREN WITH WRITING

Any assistance the parent gives the child in handwriting *after* he enters school should perhaps be done in close cooperation with the child's teacher. However, much can be done by the parent to assist the preschool child with the handwriting experience. As in any teaching situation, the parent is not expected to be an expert. Nevertheless, it is hoped that the reader might be able to make application of some of the suggestions submitted in this section of the chapter, both for the benefit of the preschool child as well as the child who has already started school. Before getting into some specific guidelines for parents, we would like to give some consideration to what is known about the handwriting of children before they enter school.

As we have inferred before, learning to read and learning to write are processes that are concerned with verbal symbols. In reading, the reader *receives* information by trying to extract meaning from the symbols, and in writing, the writer *expresses* meaning by applying the symbols with the use of combined eye-hand movements.

Although the usual sequence of language development is considered to be listening, speaking, reading, and writing, there is evidence that suggests that some children write before any formal instruction, and in some cases they write before they read. In fact, some investigators have found that writing can begin as early as three and one-half years of age, with the most prevalent time for the child's *interest* in writing beginning at age four. There are even some researchers who suggest that the teaching of handwriting precede the teaching of reading. This is based on the idea that the formation of letters, either using sets of letters or writing by hand, is the first step toward reading. It should be mentioned again, however, that the prevailing recommendation for language development still very strongly favors the sequence of listening, speaking, reading, and writing.

It has been clearly demonstrated that a *home reading environment* can have a very positive influence on the reading interest and ability of the child when he enters school. However, there has been very little investigation done with regard to *home writing environment.* Nevertheless, there appear to be certain factors in the home environment that are useful in improving the child's interest and ability in writing before he starts to school. In this particular regard, a study about *early writers* conducted by Dr. MaryAnne Hall at the University of Maryland Center for Young Children is of interest.

In this study *early writers* were defined as those children who learn to write prior to formal instruction in kindergarten and/or grade one. To be classified as such, a child's efforts at writing were to contain distinct letter and/or word forms and evidence that the child was trying to communicate or represent specific letters, words, or ideas through writing. Further, the child was expected to show continued interest in writing and engage in self-initiated writing activities on a number of occasions.

All parents reported frequent observations of the children (early writers) of one or both parents and/or brothers and sisters engaging in writing activities. In addition, all parents reported that writing materials were easily accessible to the child, usually without parental permission. (Remember our previous comment about this.) In every case, books were available, and in only one instance was it reported that newspapers and magazines were *not* available. Every one of the parents indicated that the children enjoyed being "read to" and that there was frequent observation by children of family members engaged in reading activities.

The two major conclusions made from this study were that (1) learning to write in the preschool years does occur for some children in homes that offer exposure to and models of writing in natural settings, and (2) the majority of early writers showed interest in and ability to write prior to learning to read.

With all of the above comments serving as a background of information, the following guidelines are submitted for the reader's consideration.

1. There are many different ways that a child holds a pencil. The general recommendation is that the child should hold it with the index finger and thumb, with the pencil resting on the middle finger and where the index finger and thumb meet. This position makes the pencil an extension of the forearm. If the child cannot hold the pencil in position, it may mean that he has not yet developed sufficient small muscle control. This control, which begins in the larger back and shoulder muscles, can be improved by encouraging the child to do things to improve such development. Such popular child activities as swinging and climbing are important to such development.

2. Proper placement of writing paper is very important. The child can sit in a chair with his back straight. The next step is to have him interlock his fingers, folding his hands on the table in front of him. His joined hands form a triangle with the front part of his upper body. The paper is then placed under the writing hand. For right-handed children the head is turned slightly to the left, with the opposite position for

left-handed children.

3. If your child is left-handed there might be a slight variation from the right-handed child in the use of paper and pencil. He may need to turn the paper slightly to the left, and he should hold the pencil in such a way that he can see what he is writing. It should be recognized that for a left-handed child, right to left is a more natural movement. He can be told that he always starts to write on the same side of the paper as that of his writing hand. (We have already mentioned the importance of placement when both left- and right-handed children are involved.)

4. A child may have difficulty making strokes from top to bottom (as shown in the section on writing readiness skills). If this is the case, we have found it helpful with some children to have them practice swinging their arms from front to back and from side to side. The purpose of this is to help the child develop a feeling of rhythmic movement.

5. Practically all children enjoy finger painting, and this experience can be helpful to the child in his beginning-to-write activities. With the finger painting process he can get the feel of letter formations by making circles, parts of circles, and lines. After this experience the same can be tried with a pencil.

6. With some children, when they are beginning to form letters, it is a good practice to associate the letter with something to arouse the child's interest. For example, an *O* is round like an orange, or an *S* is curled like a worm.

7. A practice that we call "talk writing" can be used with success. This involves having the child "say" the action as he forms a letter. For example, in forming an upper case *L*, you could have him say "down" as he makes the vertical stroke downward and "across" as he makes the horizontal stroke.

8. You can make a part of a letter and then have the child complete it. You also can have the child make a part of a letter and you can complete it.

9. If there is a typewriter in the home, allow the child to experiment with it. This experience can be very enjoyable for the child, and it can help with small muscle control problems if

they exist.

ACTIVE PLAY EXPERIENCES INVOLVING WRITING

Since handwriting is more or less restricted to a combination of fine muscle manipulations and eye movements, there are not as many opportunities for active play experiences in writing as there are in reading and mathematics. However, those possibilities which are available through active play are very effective.

Writing About Active Play Experiences

One of the most important factors in the beginning writing experiences of children is that these experiences involve functional situations. There is wholehearted agreement among experts on the subject that emphasis should be placed upon the using of writing in daily living in relation to the real interests and concerns of children. Probably without exception, educators are subscribing to the idea that the child's ability to express himself well in writing grows with the development of interests and the concerns that he is eager to express.

In view of modern procedures that emphasize written expression as a very important part of the child's school experience, it becomes essential that opportunities be provided for children to write in purposeful and meaningful situations. Certainly, one of the most meaningful experiences for the child (perhaps *the most meaningful*) is that which is derived from active play.

One of the ways that a parent can help the child to write about an active play experience is to use any of the activities appearing in the preceding chapters. The first step is to have the child tell about the activity after having been engaged in it. This is known as *dictating* the experience. The child's comments are dictated to the parent who, in turn, records them on a large sheet of paper or piece of cardboard. The child observes as this is being done. The parent then goes through the child's "message" with him, and they read it aloud together. The next step is to have the child write about the experience by copying what the parent has recorded. This provides a great deal of motivation for the child to write because he is able to express in writing the enjoyable experience in which he engaged.

Another approach in writing about active play experiences is to use the prepared stories in Chapters Five and Six. In addition to having the child try to read the story after having engaged in the activity depicted in the story, he can be asked to copy the story as well.

We have conducted many experiments with the above procedures. It has been found that when children engage in this type of writing activity the formation of letters (legibility) is much better than when they are asked to form letters into words under other kinds of conditions.

Body Letters

To form a letter it is important that the child develop a memory of the shape of the letter. Using the body or some of its parts to form letters can improve upon *visualization*. In Chapter Four we described this term as involving visual image, which is the mental reconstruction of a visual experience, or the result of mentally combining a number of visual experiences.

There are many ways that body letters can be formed. For example, the letter *c* can be formed with the child in a sitting position on the floor. He bends forward at the waist, bows his head, and stretches his arms forward. The letter *c* can also be formed with parts of the body. The index finger and thumb can be curled to make a *c*, or both arms can be used for a *c* by simply holding the arms to the side and bending them at the elbows.

The creative parent in collaboration with the child will be able to work out numerous other body letter possibilities. It is a good practice to have both the child and the parent form a body letter and then have the other guess what the letter is.

Big Pencil

When a child begins to form letters he should be provided the opportunity to do this in several ways. One way is for him to pretend that he is a *big pencil*. He becomes a big pencil by first standing with his hands joined in front of him. Next, he bends forward with his arms straight and his joined hands pointing toward the floor. The parent calls out a letter and/or shows the child a large letter written in manuscript. The child goes through the movement of forming the letter by moving his joined hands as if he were a pencil.

Action Word Writing

For action word writing the parent will need to prepare materials as follows. Cut heavy cardboard (white tag board is preferred) into several pieces about 6 inches wide and 12 inches long. Such action words as *jump, hop,* and *run* are written in manuscript on one side of the card. The cards are placed in a pile a given distance away from the child. At a signal he runs to the pile of cards. He selects one card, does what it says, and returns to this original position. For example, if it says "jump," he takes several jumps back to where he started. When he returns, he copies the word on a piece of paper and returns for another card. If desired, the activity can be timed to see how much the child improves each time the activity is played.

In closing this final chapter, we would like to emphasize again that the active play medium of learning has been thoroughly tested and has proved very satisfactory as a most desirable way of learning for young children. Over 175 active play learning experiences have been provided, and creative parents will no doubt be able to make up others to use to help their children learn.

Not only does this approach provide excellent opportunities for children to learn and improve their abilities in the 3R's, but at the same time very enjoyable parent-child relationships can be expected to be forthcoming. The whole idea of this procedure may have been summarized best by Prince Otto von Bismarck back in the nineteenth century when he commented that *you can do anything with children if you only play with them.*

INDEX